Paging Doctor Jazz

Typeset and printed by Q3 Print Project Management Ltd,
Loughborough, Leicestershire.
(01509) 213456

Published by Shoestring Press
19 Devonshire Avenue, Beeston, Nottingham, NG9 1BS
(0115) 925 1827
www.shoestringpress.co.uk

First published 2004

ISBN: 1 904886 08 6

Paging Doctor Jazz

A Verse Anthology

Compiled and with an Introduction by
John Lucas

Shoestring Press

Introduction

News of Jazz reached these shores sometime before the Great War began, though it was only during the years 1914–18 that the music began to acquire cult status, especially among the young. For soldiers going off to the trenches, the opportunity to dance to rhythms that were as frenzied as they were expressive of the new machine age had an undeniable allure, especially as the dance steps that went with them implied the energy of sexual licence which is connected to one of the root meanings of jazz. This at all events is how the popularity of jazz among the war-time young has been explained by any number of social historians. The "young" in question are for the most part southern — the dancing was virtually confined to London hotels and restaurants — and officer class. And then there were the drugs. Opium and cocaine were easily come by and, with drink, became linked to the "devil's music", as jazz was not infrequently called.

More frequently still, or more persuasively, jazz was soon labelled "decadent". Quite how much this had to do with its being music made by black people I'm not sure, though there is little doubt that racism, unconscious or otherwise, underlies much of the hostility to jazz expressed by writers during the 20s and 30s. It wasn't just writers of course. When the young Sidney Bechet visited England in 1919 as a featured virtuoso with Will Marion Cook's Orchestra and Choir, he soon attracted the attention of local musicians and aficianados of the new music. Following its not hugely successful tour of Europe, the orchestra returned to the USA, but Bechet stayed on in London. (Until he was deported in November, 1922, having served a short prison sentence for "unlawful assault" — he was involved in a brawl that included a woman who may or may not have been a prostitute.) But like other visiting black musicians both then and later Bechet found difficulty in obtaining lodgings. I don't know when or where jazz was first called "jungle music", but the implications of the soubriquet, much used in the 1920s, are plain.

In 1924, T.S. Eliot paid a visit to Arnold Bennett. He wanted, so Bennett recorded in his Journal, to write "a drama of modern life (furnished-flat sort of people) in a rhythmical prose 'perhaps with certain things in it accentuated by drum beats.'" The result presumably is *Sweeney Agonistes* with its parodic use of popular songs that abut on jazz: "*Under the bamboo/Bamboo bamboo/Under the bamboo tree.*" And already, in the *Waste land*, Eliot had identified the death of culture with jazz: "O O O O that Shakespeherian Rag —/It's so elegant/So intelligent." Jazz was the music of the damned, of furnished-flat sort of people, of people with no roots. Alternatively it went with fast cars, fast music and fast girls. All those vile bodies speeding to destruction. In Noel Coward's *The Vortex*, first performed in 1924, the play's anti-hero, Nicky, identifies his own sense of despair when, according to a stage direction, "He goes to the piano and begins to play jazz". But jazz was also portable music, a matter of ukeleles and wind-up gramophones. The spreading menace was signalled by newspaper headlines of the time. "*WELSH INVOKE CURFEW LAWS AS ONE WAY TO STOP JAZZ.*"

Flip this upside down, though, and jazz becomes the music of conscious transgression: deliberately shocking, liberating, part of the revolt of the young against the old, and even to be recruited for radical or anyway protest politics. Marches of the unemployed in the 1920s were frequently led by what were called jazz bands. These were usually put together from a combination of kazoos, paper-and-comb, and snare drums, and the music rarely strayed far from popular songs and hymn tunes. Nothing wrong with that, of course, and indeed both instrumentation and choice of music were common enough in the early days of jazz. But "jazz" here means music of protest as it did during the miners' strike of 1984/5, when yet again "jazz bands", this time predominantly made up of children, led marchers through the streets of mining communities in the North of England.

This identification of jazz with radical politics may help to explain the disdain in which it was held by certain writers in the 1920s. If so, you'd think that this would guarantee its appeal to writers of the 1930s. Not a bit of it. For them, jazz was like the cinema: a cheap drug calculated to turn into mindless zombies those who fell for its meretricious charms. Hence George

Thomson, in *Marxism and Poetry*, takes for granted the evils of "jazz and other forms of commercialised music." In fairness to Thomson, who as well as being a marxist was the greatest classical scholar of his generation, I should add that he and his wife, the Mozart scholar Katherine Thomson, organised between them the Clarion Choir, with which they toured back-of-the-lorry performances of Mozart operas round and about the Birmingham area during the 1930s. A great and good man, certainly, but why didn't it ever occur to Thomson that Mozart's was a "commercialised music", although to say as much is to say very little. It certainly tells you nothing about the music itself, any more than condemning jazz as "commercialised" tells you anything useful about music whose greatest as well as least creators often played for a pittance.

During the1930s jazz was, however, sympathetically written about by a number of musicologists, among them Constant Lambert. In an important passage in his *Music Ho!* (1934), Lambert praises certain records of Duke Ellington for "the amazingly skilful proportions" of their colour. "I know of nothing in Ravel so dextrous in treatment as the varied solos in the middle of the ebullient *Hot and Bothered* and nothing in Stravinsky more dynamic than the final section... The exquisitely tired and four-in-the-morning *Mood Indigo* is an equally remarkable piece of writing." And in "Tell Me the Truth About Love" Auden, that most eclectric of poets, makes good use of the kind of lyric developed by jazz-inflected Cole Porter. He also includes a number of blues, drug songs and spirituals in his two great anthologies of the decade, *The Oxford Book of Light Verse* and *The Poet's Tongue*.

Auden may, like Lambert, have listened to jazz on record. From the middle of the decade it was far less easy to listen to the great jazz musicians themselves, because the UK Musicians Union slapped a ban on individual American performers which prevented them from bringing their own groups to the UK. If they wanted backing musicians — and who didn't? —, they had to use the musicians registered with the UK Union. So, for example, when Fats Waller visited in 1938, his "Rhythm" lacked any of Herman Autrey, Gene Sedrick or Zutty Singleton. Not that this would have bothered his many admirers here, because they continued to know his work less from live performances than from records. And as the 30s wore on, more and more recorded jazz was made available to British listeners. As one of them later recalled, "Sitting with a friend in his bedroom that overlooked the family tennis-court, I watched leaves drift down through long Sunday afternoons as we took it in turn to wind the portable HMV, and those white and coloured Americans, Bubber Miley, Frank Tessmacher, J.C. Higginbotham, spoke immediately to our understanding." Thus Philip Larkin, remembering adolescent years in the English midlands, and his experience was, as he noted, being replicated in houses across Britain. The result was that the generation to which Larkin, Kingsley Amis and John Wain belonged, was the first that would choose to celebrate the music rather than using jazz as a marker of society's ills.

I suspect such celebration must have gained an added zest from the presence here during the war of American GIs, some of whom were professional jazz musicians, others of whom brought jazz records with them and played them at the dances organised for them up and down the land. Moreover, the American contribution to the liberation of Europe from Nazism not only went with a swing, but swing itself was inseparable from the hopes, the exuberant energies released by the lifting of dread. What better expression of the meaning of D-day than "In the Mood"? It is one of the nicer points of the history of the music that in the same year Glenn Miller recorded that number, Charlie Parker went into the Savoy studios to record "Tiny's Tempo" and "Red Cross", two tracks that as Ross Russell says in his sympathetic biography of Parker, *Bird Lives*, "became the foundation stone of every modern jazz record collection."

These tracks would not however have featured in Larkin's collection. For Larkin, Parker notoriously formed one of a trinity of loathed Ps. (The others were Picasso and Pound.) It's a strange feature of Larkin's way of writing about jazz, a music which after all starts in the 20th century, and which is associated with much that's particular to it, that he makes it seem positively venerable.

"I shall, I suppose, always remember.../ The flock of notes those antique negroes blew/Out of Chicago air into/ A huge remembering pre-electric horn". The lines come from "Reference Back", a poem Larkin wrote in 1955, when the record in question, King Oliver's "Riverside Blues", was scarcely more than thirty years old. To identify such music as "pre-electric" is however to make it seem positively antedeluvian. And fancy calling musicians, some of whom were still alive at the time Larkin wrote the poem, "antique negroes." What on earth is he up to, transforming them into a kind of pastoral, elegising them as a lost way of life? The answer is obvious.

Between the happy highway of then and now looms Modernism, in jazz as in all else. That Larkin was not alone in this view of the matter can be gauged from an incident that dates from three years earlier, when Humphrey Lyttleton's band turned up for a gig at Birmingham Town Hall to find themselves confronted by a banner directed at the alto-saxophonist Bruce Turner, who had recently joined the outfit. GO HOME DIRTY BOPPER it said. Never mind that among the great exponents of the instrument was Johny Hodges. An alto saxophone now meant Charlie Parker.

Forward to 1955 again. By then I had bought my first trumpet and was playing in a group which a music newspaper characterised with pitiless accuracy as "a first-class third-class band." At one gig a youth of about our age, dressed in full teddy boy regalia, asked if he could sit in with us. Of course. He produced an alto-sax, nominated "Cherokee", and brought it in at such lightning speed that none of us could hope to stay with him. It wasn't our kind of music, we told ourselves afterwards. We were less ready to admit that he was our technical superior. The audience didn't like what he played, they were there to dance rather than to listen, and you certainly couldn't dance to his music. After he had finished, he packed away his instrument and left, and we went back to our standard fare of music from New Orleans to Chicago, music that was popular with the punters.

Popular. The word needs to be handled with caution. If you except the horrid "traddy-pop" boom which lasted no more than two years, jazz was never, I think, truly popular music in the UK, although in the 1950s, when there were jazz clubs and venues aplenty where the music could be heard and danced to, it was bebop's pronounced unpopularity on the dance floor that lent it privileged status for some musicians and their fans. They dressed up for their music: suits, button-down collars, or ted gear. Traditionalists dressed down: check shirts, cords. But there's no point in trying to make this into a matter of class. There were middle-class boppers and working-class ravers and vice versa. Only one type of follower came from a single stratum. Hooray Henries, whether male or female, were always upper class. I'm slightly surprised that no poem I've come across deals with this matter, but perhaps it's as well. Far better to concentrate on the music itself. There are quite enough good poems about the various forms of jazz and the people who played and sang (and play and sing) to warrant an anthology. And, as Fats would say. "here 'tis, then."

A NOTE ON THE ORDER OF CONTENTS

When I began thinking of this anthology some years ago I intended it to be the hundredth publication of Shoestring Press. In the event, I've gone some way past that number, but *Paging Doctor Jazz* is nevertheless an enterprise dear to my heart, a celebration of the two art forms that have meant and continue to mean most to me. From the start I was clear that the anthology would include poems by poets on this side of the Atlantic alone. This was less because I knew I could never afford American permission fees than because I wanted the anthology to retain a certain focus. But just how to achieve this became something of a headache. I spent a good deal of time dithering about the best, or least unsatisfactory, ordering of the contents. Should I follow the history of jazz itself, begin with poems about spirituals and early blues, and come as far up to date as the poems I had at my disposal permitted? But then all the poems about musicians and groups from the earlier periods would have to be huddled together, and this would do violence to sequences by individual poets, among them Michael Longley, Neil Powell and George Szirtes, which brought together musicians from different periods. Alphabetically, by musician then? No, boring. Then how about going by instrument? But this would have drawn attention to the fact that jazz drummers get a raw deal, that few love a bass player, and that everyone loves Fats Waller. (Quite right, too.) In the end, I thought it better to proceed alphabetically by poet. There is a wondrous photograph of jazz musicians of all ages and from every conceivable jazz preference who happened to be in Harlem on a day in 1958 when Art Kane had the idea of bringing them together in order to point his camera at them. As a result, some fairly unlikely musicians rub shoulders. In the pages that follow Freddie Green is close to Albert Ayler, which neither would probably mind, and Acker Bilk stands next to Chet Baker, an arrangement to which the latter might well object. No matter. Feel free to open the anthology wherever you choose. You're sure to be paging Doctor Jazz.

John Lucas

Contents

Hello, Central…

SONNY ROLLINS ON THE WILLIAMSBURG BRIDGE

In the middle of the dark wood
of his life a man might decide
that a change of direction is what's required,

and take to going out nights
onto the Williamsburg Bridge where Manhattan's lights
are a glittery sheen that skates

on the East River –
and sit among the noise and glare
playing the saxophone for whoever.

He blows variations
on *St. Thomas, Body & Soul*, but no-one really listens,
except maybe the Brooklyn trains

that shuffle in four,
ferrying souls over the dark water,
a back-beat to the singular encounter

of breath and air,
which anyone there
would tell you is a person's only true career.

C J Allen

FAREWELL BLUES

Bongo, sitar, 'cello, flute, electric piano, bass guitar,
Training Orchestra, Research Team, Workshop,
   Group, Conservatoire,
Square Root, Nexus, Barbaresque, Distortions,
   Voltage – bloody row,
For Louis Armstrong, Mildred Bailey, Walter Page
and Sidney Catlett lie in Brunwick churchyard
now.

Trumpets gelded, drums contingent, saxophones
   that bleat or bawl,
Keyless, barless, poor-man's Boulez, improvising
   on fuck-all,
Far beyond what feeling, reason, even mother wit
   allow,
While Muggsy Spanier, Floyd O'Brien, Sterling
   Bose and Henry Allen lie in Decca churchyard
   now.

Dead's the note we loved that swelled within us,
   made us gasp and stare.
Simple joy and simple sadness thrashing the
   astounded air;
What replaced them no one asked for, but it turned
   up anyhow,
And Coleman Hawkins, Johnny Hodges, Bessie
   Smith and Pee Wee Russell lie in Okeh churchyard
   now.

Kingsley Amis

MELLY

Something sad about clowns;
something thin between laughter and tears.
Pity the dignity, the love and the hate,
the twitching wire between body and soul
and you on that stage,
drunk on rum and borrowed blues again;
unique in the balance you keep to yourself –
never quite losing it,
never quite making it;
bawling out between Magritte and Morton,
playing the droopy-drawered clown
with yourself,
you

do the Melly-Belly,
the Ovaltine,
big brash belly-laugh blues.

Keith Armstrong

POEM FOR A BLUES HARMONICA
(for Ad van Emmerik)

A poem is an organ of the mouth,
a verse I suck and blow.
It sings from my heart on the wind,
it breathes with my life.

I place my poetry between my lips,
like licking my girl-friend's breasts.
I smoke it like a cigar
and squeeze the good juice from it.

My poetry is a fire,
it screams blues murders.
I craft it with my gentle fingers
and shout it around the world.

This poem is a drink wet with rhyme,
a harp in a rowdy beer museum.
I am a drunk whose rhymes stagger,
my words are music in your ear.

Keith Armstrong

CLOSE ENOUGH FOR JAZZ

When
 the music starts
 with just a walking bass
 and rhythm struts like melody
 till melody swings in;

When
 the beat is dancing
 round the corners of a square
 and we know that we're inside
 a tight small box together;

When
 you pull back like a sudden wave
 and leave me riding high on silence
 then wrongfoot me with a shuffle
 to make my pulse rise to my throat;

And when
 I bend the string you least expect;
 or we climb a key change
 that would surely pin an audience
 to their chair backs;

Then
 our eyes engage
 and we understand again
 why lovers look at one another
 like musicians.

Michael Bartholomew-Biggs

MILES

There is frost on the verges
and he is playing *Summertime.*
Each note unwinds the road a hundred yards
in the film that's showing on my windscreen.

In front of the camera
I have wanted, many times,
to be the one who changed the storyline,
and played a scene the way it wasn't written.

To accept I'm an extra
is getting easier each time
directors keep the take the star ad-libbed
and choose instead to cut and splice the seasons.

Michael Bartholomew-Biggs

THREE FOR THE DUKE

Sophisticated Lady
Years from the Storyville of booze and whores,
these lovely ladies sipping wine
in a concert interval are glad
the noise is done.
The men compete — discographies
and edit numbers, long-forgotten names
who gigged with Bix in '24—
they solo in the spotlight of the lore;
But when the band swings into *Satin Doll*,
the satin's all they see; the empty glamour
of the doll is lost on them,
her shining desolation.

Caravan

The lights are up at last. The dirty air
is mostly smoke. The hall is once again a hall,
the ceiling overhead, where it had seemed
the stars to which the music's inspiration rose.
In brassy light the band packs lifeless instruments
in scruffy cases, talking of girls and mortgages.
Now, who would know these men had made this room
another universe, and would work
familiar magic in another room,
once they'd moved on.

Stormy Weather

Can't go on …
Ice tinkles in the gins,
this foreign beer's the business, don't you know!
The knives and forks knit and clink and
… every thing I had is gone
Now it's the car, and over by the door
the central heating's on the blink,
and no-one hears the rain pink on the glass,
above the noise. The song ends,
but the storm goes on.

Roger Burford Mason

FASCINATING RHYTHM, 1953

Dublin, Sunday morning, September,
and I wander through the quiet streets,
trying to keep myself awake
after an all-night crossing of the Irish Sea.
I can still feel the rhythm
as the ship hit the rise and fall of the waves,
still hear the urgent voices
talking about now-forgotten records.

And later the same day, a theatre in the city,
the excitement as Zoot Sims
strolls to the microphone, raises his tenor,
and starts the first solo of the concert.
Stan Kenton smiling, all tiredness gone,
no thought of the long journey home.
Nothing but the rhythm,
and the rise and fall of music in my memory.

Jim Burns

AGAINST THE SQUARE WORLD

"Listen", I said, "I shook Red Rodney's hand,
talked to Dexter Gordon, and had my photograph
taken with the great Joe Albany".

"Nobody knows about those people any more",
she replied, and I said, "So the world is full
of squares, but I remember their names,

and what they did. The music they made
still runs through my head every day.
A square world can't make magic go away".

Jim Burns

THOSE OLD JAZZ PHOTOGRAPHS

Hey, look at them there, hair
slicked down on either side
of their heads, and holding
their horns as if they were
going to hurl them at us any
moment. Wow, what music they
must have played, way back
in the Jazz Decade. I can
almost hear it now, that tight
rhythm, and those hot licks,
and the smooth-toned singers
slipping sweetly through, "Tea
for Two" and "Exactly Like You".
I wonder where they are now?
America must be full of old men,
living in rooms with greasy suits
hung behind the doors, and waiting
for someone to ask them if they
ever bought Beiderbecke a beer.

Jim Burns

SCRAPPLE FROM THE APPLE

East Side, West Side,
all around the town,
the hipsters said, "Bird lives",
even wrote it down

on the subway walls,
in the canyons of steel,
as they hustled for a living,
a fix for their next meal.

Dewey Square to 52nd Street,
black circles spinning around;
the hipsters are all dead now,
Bird lives in his sound.

Jim Burns

THE AGEING HIPSTER'S DREAM

All those popular songs of the period,
sung by thin-faced crooners in evening
suits, backed by groups of bored-looking
musicians, the middle-aged men thinking,
"It's a hell of a way of making a living,
weeks away from the wife and kids," and
the younger ones holding their saxes like
Lester, and wondering if Woody or someone
will ever ask them to join *the* band.
And there I am, in a blue drape-suit and
knitted tie, hunched in front of the
stand, sneering at the dancers, and
waiting for the hip-looking tenorman

to take a solo, so I can shout "Go", and
we'll all be gone, and the moment will
be fixed, and the sound and the scene
always remain the same. Cool. So very cool.

Jim Burns

THREE JAZZ SOLOS

A Stan Getz Solo

Show time, and neat gin
entices the zax soloist,
tuneful and nimble.

Great event, tenorwise –
zinging, swinging towards a nervy,
golden evening, totally zany.

Start the action now!
Getz's entered tarassic zones!

Stan, transform all neurotics:
God, excuse their zeal:
Squares, try a nightclub,
gently enter the zoo!

A Spat For Miles Davis

Music inspires love, Esther sings
devotedly at Vince.

Instantly, Simon moves inside
leaving Esther suddenly devastated.

Angry, Vince insists Simon's melophobia
insults lovely Esther.

Stubborn, denying a volte-face,
immovable Simon mooches indoors

lazily eating satsumas,
declaring archly, *vocals inflict suffering.*

Chet Baker Goes East

Chin Ho enters the busy atrium,
kismet expectant.

Rhoda can't help eyeing
the boy's artful kabaya.

Even Roy's charmed.
How entrancing, the boy's appeal.

Kris-like, envy rises.

Chin Ho eschews the British, always –
knee-jerking, emotive response, certainly.

However, experience teaches Brits
are kinkily erotic rascals!

Derrick Buttress

MEMORIES OF A JAZZ AGE

I
Jazz from the Roseland,
the Frog Hop and Connie's Inn –
Jam in Hell's Kitchen.

Midnight in the Green Cat,
breakfast of ribs in Arcadia,
sleep through whiskey dreams.

Speakeasy nights
swinging in the Bucket of Blood
with the Lion of Judaea.

The guy on cornet's
flying high on bathtub gin.
Up there – perfect sound!

II

Everybody loved Bix.
The boy from Davenport
didn't have an enemy in the world.
But he was out of this world most of the time.

Music was all he lived for.
He wanted to do more with music
than any man possibly could.
He made it beautiful as well as hot.

But the darkness was closing in,
and he didn't seem to care.
Part of him was in the dark already.

III

Then there was Bunk Johnson,
Buster Bailey and Alphonse Picou
with those *Milneberg Joys*,
the creole girls dancing the *Shim-Me-Sha-Wobble*

Remember Bubber Miley with Tricky Sam Nanton
travelling the *East St Louis Toodle-Oo*?
Buddy Bolden, now, *Didn't He Ramble*
in that *Honky-Tonk Town*
while he waited for *One Sweet Letter From You,*
Pretty Baby, Rose of the Rio Grande?

Oh Make Me a Pallet on the Floor –
I've Got a Feeling I'm Falling,
falling as far as the King of New Orleans,
as deep as the *Dead Man Blues.*

Derrick Buttress

SONG OF THE OLD HEP-CAT

Well, flatten my fifth and call me cool,
I'm just a kid from the bebop school.

Put me on that old 'A' train,
I want to hear the Duke again.

Unlock my soul with your E flat key,
Lady Day's torch is burning for me.

Hit me hard with that laid-back beat,
The Red Bank kid's swinging down the street.

Mellow my horn with a plunger mute,
blow those moths from my old zoot suit.

Sharpen my F and call me G,
that sweet trombone's by Tommy D.

Dazzle me Louis with a blue Hot Five,
got my zimmer and I'm ready to jive.

Derrick Buttress

NEW ORLEANS JAZZ, 1910
(After "Hear Me Talkin' To Ya"
by Nat Shapiro and Nat Hentoff)

Trumpet:
Here in Storyville where the party
never ends, do not disdain
Miss Albertine McKay's hot brown kiss.
Lady of the snub-nose gat,
Queen of the dum-dum slug,
she can cure the blues – and make 'em!
She's mean okay, but halfway to an angel
in the shadow of Cold Blood Jack,
the unforgiving. He spits in coffins
for luck and slyly hones
the sharpest blade in town,
rips those sailors loose from their pay
and sends them floating
on the long voyage home.

Clarinet:
If you want cut-glass chandeliers
and mirrored walls, then slip your skin
inside Miss Lulu White's house of whores,
a fine old place, built like a grand hotel.
She's run by an alligator octoroon
whose love is strictly C.O.D.
Or slide on down to Buck Tooth Rena's crib
for a taste of the honeyed trick.
For gambling action use your sporting house,
the hall of dice and three-card cotch,
dealt from the bottom, while Creole girls
strut their high-class stuff.

Side-drum:
Then you go marching home to mama.
Don't go near no clip joints now!

While one of nature's ladies
serves up juice and jive
another tip-toes through the dark
and rifles that secret pocket
in your store-bought Sunday pants.

Piano:
Sleep is for suckers.
When that magenta eve floats down
the boys and girls ride back
from the races at City Park,
sniff the whiskey on the air
and light their fine cigars.
Ready to sport, ready to jive.
Up in Countess Willie's Sporting House
Miss Big Butt Annie and Bird Leg Nora
share some hop with Joe the Pimp,
while Steel Arm John (you run
when he calls) gets ready to ramble.
The Devil's dust will lay you dead
before your time, the preacher swears,
but Storyville will set the sweetest smile
on your stone-cold, everloving face.

Ensemble:
It was like the aurora borealis,
one of those phenomenon,
only it was a sound,
a sound you couldn't fathom,
the thunder of sudden music
which sent us running, searching
through New Orleans into the Tenderloin,
so clear, so high we'd lose our breath
trying to find it:
"It's this way! It's that way!"
And you'd be no nearer that music.
But it came on again, always like that,

distant, out of reach,
the city full of music
which made you ache with love,
made you want to dance.

Derrick Buttress

GLASSBLOWER

'the thing a person plays may be the only beautiful thing in them'
(Art Farmer)

you set fire to the air

there it goes again

a giant perfect
smoke ring

amoretti paper
that keeps on
up
over

mike stands
half-dead bottles
of house red
autographs
on serviettes

into Soho air
above those last
al fresco punters
at *Bar Italia*

becoming
cut defined
pure a soul
I'd hazard

before you
detach
mouthpiece
knock it
clear of spittle

human
after all

Peter Carpenter

UNDERCURRENT

I never get much further than the end
of track two, the second take of 'My Funny Valentine'
and it's usually played as a cheddar mash
is being prepared for chicken with that balsamic vinegar
and honey sauce or I'm chucking a salad together
capricciosa. The ancient beatbox atop the fridge
sometimes skims on or sticks but no matter
when it's you and me, my dear, the children just about in bed.

Those first six notes of Bill Evans' virtuoso piano
and Jim Hall's 'stop-and-go' guitar, as the sleeve-note
puts it, keep on coming as I try to blank out my mother,
following her stay of just a few days, poor love,
and my unwarranted annoyance, my bleak anger
at her eating habits — like a horse, double dose of meringue
or cake, trilled with, why not, cream or what-have-you, killer
for the stroke-victim and late-diagnosed diabetic — or her
'that's just like the first flat we had at Barnes together'

verdict on any house with verandah or the flicker
of her touchpaper hands a twitch like caught fish
at the end of a line or right foot quivering over
phantom passenger-side brake as I overtake or indicate
to move into another lane on the A21 or the glaze
that comes over her face as we try to get real
about the future and the loneliness of her daily rountine.

And this little duet has the right blend of 'wistful melancholy'
and 'rhythmic precision' to be given its own sleeve-notes,
I'm thinking, were anyone madly attentive enough
to precise delivery over the years, the muttered explosions
at nothing, the as-ever-unresolvable attrition
of fret and string, its exended intermodulation,
its staggering shifts in tempo and expression, until the machine
blips us forward into the alternate take of 'Romain'.

Peter Carpenter

FOR A CORNET PLAYER, RETIRED

So: no more Sister Kate
Perdido Street
or Limehouse Blues

no again Downhearted
Swing Parade or
Gatemouth, Darktown

won't play Somebody Stole
My Gal (Weeping
Willow Blues) or

Ory's Creole Trombone
will not return
to Tight Like That

and what of Empty Bed
Blues? After You've
Gone? Got No Blues?

But you'll still hear, hidden
in your waking dreams
those Farewell Blues.

Barry Cole

WAY DOWN YONDER IN NEW ORLEANS

Lunch-time on Bourbon Street,
The five-piece in the bar
Blares *Way down yonder*
To attract customers for juleps,
Beers or Irish coffees.
Volume's the thing.
A crumpled veteran on clarinet
Heaves to his feet
To take his spot and fluffed
And dirty notes fall as far
From ones he could have played
As youth and pristine dreams.
Obligatory applause,
Enhanced by booze,
Slews off him as he sits
Hunched-shouldered staring at the floor.
Later his hang-dog eyes catch mine
Confirming that he knows.

I know, they say, what's dead,
And you are dying with me.
Truth's revelation?
He puts out his tongue,
A signal to the barman.
It's thirst we're dying of.

John Cotton

JAZZ IN NEW JERSEY

For Pat & Sandy Maxwell

We turn off the Turnpike
And out of the night
Into an explosion of noise and light
At the Chester Inn,
Where for the evening,
proclaimed by banners,
BIX LIVES in trumpet and trombone.
During a break the band joins us for drinks.
'Meet Joe, he'll just love someone new
To tell his stories to'.
'Say, you're from England? Tell me,
Is the Corner House, Marble Arch still there?
Played tuba at the opening in 1923'.
What do I tell him of it now?
After all, it's his reality,
As someday, this may well be mine.

John Cotton

THE MUSICIANS

At three o'clock, the dead hour of the day,
the uninvited audience away,
severally, we fit reeds, tune strings; speak
with tube or sound-board; matters of technique.

It happens that, at night, returning home
unsatisfied, or angry, drunken, some
one of us may take, say, clarinet,
and serenade the sleeping street: regret
his impulse in the morning, finding
the instrument in the kitchen, hearing

neighbours call "We heard you! Very nice!"
Once in a while. We tolerate this vice.

What we condemn is — playing to the moon,
acceding to facile "Give us a tune!",
surrendering to socializers' hearty
cajolings, "Bring your guitar to the party!"

Austere, unentertaining, is our way.
We are preparing; there will come a day
that we must learn to know. Then we shall say
"Now is our time. For this we learnt to play".

Simon Darragh

THE JAZZ ORCHESTRA

One

Swinging chintz, blues of a jiggered spinster
My sister? I haven't got a sister
At fifty-five it's mad to think of her …
My secret fan, that foot-tap in the dark.

Two

Cloth ears in Soho and the 1950s.
I dream of scissors.
I read *The Carpetbaggers* as I play
'Dancing in the Dark', 'Hernando's Hideaway'.
In ballrooms of the North, middle-aged
Romancers of their pasts, tastes formed,
Like mine, in an estaminet of Manchester,
Sing to the 'Sunset Serenade'.
Their superannuation's theme-song.
I ended up bitter. Like this.

Three

'The first cigarette of the day'
Up all night, dawn was a taxi
In our American suits, my Lester hat
My pocket full of reeds
Our carnal contact and our job
I dream myself black at the Blue Note
And by my dedication, deleted
Morning's kiosks
A double-bass on the platform of a first bus
One fat passenger
Music with no home to go to

Four

Playing Guiffre's 'Four Brothers'
We regret there are only three of us
The fourth pal gave up learning his chords
And works every night for a fortune

Five

My long blonde hair updates them thirty years
I sit behind them, the bugger beat
An octopus in love
I don't want dreams or black women
Or these famous names they hug
Obsolete shit, too much technique
Too many crew-cuts
Fingers fatten round their rings
They lost the knack of clothes and presentation

I plan myself away to the suave accountant
The guy who says
"I am the last of the old smoothies".

Six

We work under the benediction
Of a single feather, and Parker plays
On a skyline of diners
His art of razored cane

Seven

Venery of saxophones, 'the woman-killer'
Giver of lady-sweat
Soap and nylon, the kissed cosmetic
Body-dew, good time fragrances
Mythical love affair with the instrument
More than that
It opens up the voice from where it rises
Deep, in intestinal secrets,
Abdomenal, vascular, thoracic.

Eight

"Gutter Gershwins", the lady said,
"They are Gutter Gershwins,
With, of course, the prominent exceptions
Of Mr. Goodman, Mr. Shaw and Mr. Herman,
All of whom excite, dress well, and do not offend".

"Jesus *Shit*!" cried Mr. Parker. "Now then.
Now *then*! Go get me a *small* dead bat.
With that under my chin, I'll look,
At least I'll *look*, like a saxophone player".

But it did no good. Not to Bird
And not to John Coltrane.
Look, Listen! shout the fluent changes.
We play the air and urban rain
For nothing or for scale or more than scale.

Our fame cries out its own acknowledgements.
We transcended our skins, and paid for it.

Nine

The taste in the brain
After nightmare
She will steal your records
And leave her ash all over the place
She's left her underwear in many bedrooms
Good riddance to the thief
Our legendary girlfriend's gone
Some kid might be practicing on
My horn she hocked
You have to start on a stolen horn
From where someone left off
The night is full of borrowed horns
Their lips on my lips
Jazz is an engine of lips and hands
Ritual feet shuffle and count
Flying home

Ten

St. Cecilia's concentration camp
Is full of jazzmen, wearing numbers
Here is the almanac of musical chances
The chance the sun might rise, the chance
Small change might drop into your hat

Blue beggars, blow!

Eleven

Young enough to have no need of hope
They play and play their present time
They think is their contemporary

In the view from the hot-dog stand
Crushed wrappers twitch
Outside the auditorium
And Mr. Amplified electrocutes
A future of musical instruments
The sound of instruments is patronized
It is not on 'the charts'
These sounds are called 'instrumentals'
Long ago, there were no quick philosophies
Once upon a time, music was big and round
Men played their lives away
And wore their mouths or fingers out
Until all you could hear
Was a heart and a mind
Clever grief, sad elation
Intricate, intricate, simple
The way all things should be

Twelve

New elegance is stranger than most
Social phenomena, summing up
Nerves of an era in a fad.
Just as clothes become us,
And our voices own new words
We picked up without knowing it,
This is a strange art, reluctant
To be called such, or this, or that.

Lester Young made elegance.
His music flowed, a cruel nylon
From an instrument, a cry of alcohol.
Like poetry, the saddest turn in showbiz.

W.H. Auden used to practice walking like the stars,
Lighting a cigarette like Bogart.
It didn't pass him by either.

Having invented an era,
Lester Young died, but said
To Buddy Tate some weeks before —
"Lady Tate, I guess they never liked my horn, did they?"
Lots of people don't like when they live.

Thirteen

Ellington at the keyboard
And it is suave, the sound
Of *savoir vivre* saddened
The wit of travelling on night-trains

Orchestra
Musical instruments
The full sense of terms
Genuis Ghetto Fame

Douglas Dunn

BILLIE 'N' ME

You could never have been a friend of mine,
Even if I played as sweet as dead Lester
Three feet from you, because you mean too much,
Your voice opens all doors on fed-up love.

There were dreams of you, in the ideal night club,
The members gone, just you, the band, and me
In my white tuxedo resisting requests to leave,
Then walking back to my pampered hotel room

In a dawn of fanciful New York heights,
Wondering how you'd take my roses sent at noon,
The invitation to lunch, that you ignored,
The lyrics I had written but you would not sing,

Black, dead, put down by love that was too much,
Mismanaged pleasures. And silent now
As the saxophones in Harlem pawnshops,
Your voice that meant how tough love is.

Douglas Dunn

AND ON THAT NOTE:
Jazz Elegies

Wellstood, for forty-odd years,
guessed what there was to do next
and did it. Tipped
the history of the art half over
and went in where it suited;
and understanding that music's
more about movement than structure
proceeded to lurch, stamp,
splash, caper, grumble, sprint,
bump and trudge — mostly
on the piano – then sat down
in his hotel room before dinner
and, too soon, stopped.

Strange channels for new noises. That steely-eyed
old man, dapper,
sugar-coated in famous vanity
and endless glad-handing,
carried always somewhere about him
what he'd come upon early, a monstrous,
husky, thoroughly dangerous saxophone sound
never before heard on earth;

and on a bandstand if you put your foot
behind him hard enough,
out it would still come honking
with no manners at all.

Three piano-players
taking turns on the portable
stool. The first
tucks it close in
and perches like a hamster, as he must.
Second, I slide it back
to make good room to slouch
as I permit myself. Finally,
gaunt and purposeful, he drags it
to the extreme: Glenn Gould
plays Crazy Horse in crimson suede
pointed boots; extensible arms
reaching for distant keys, spine curved,
navel in phobic flight from the piano. The music,
after a moment's meditation, comes streaking out
in elasticated pulses: wild, dramatic,
timeless East Eurpoean Stride

Taking care never to learn
the ways of the world till the moment
the alto would assume its insinuating angle and get
blown straight into life. Seeing a waiting audience, then
blinking awake mildly, leaning down to whisper
surprise news to the pianist: "Trouble is,
I just can't seem to remember the names of
any tunes at all. Serious problem there." Prolonged
pause, prolonged. Again, after some painful night:
"How can those people go on playing
for twenty or thirty years and never even
start to want to learn their instuments?"
Serious question there.

Ears up, neck solid,
punching pretty tunes off centre
through a stubby *cornett*: "The way I figure it,
the sound comes out
that much closer to my face, and
that's where I want it." Lovely old
American tunes, and talking: "I guess you people
must all be thinking I'm just another American
loudmouth!" Talking: "What key?
THIS key!" "What tempo?
It's a BALLAD, for Christ's sake!" On a sofa
at a party in his honour, persuaded
to toot gently and graciously for his supper,
looses off at full volume and quells
New York Town Hall, with nothing
in pursuit but my quite small piano.

Whistling in the dark,
wobbling a pallid flame down
to the bottom of the bottle:
owl-sounds, muffled
sqawks. Nothing
better to do but whistle
when there's so much dark.

This poem commemorates some musicians, now dead, I used to play with or alongside: Bud Freeman, Archie Semple, Duncan Swift, Dick Wellstood, Bruce Turner, Wild Bill Davison.

Roy Fisher

THE THING ABOUT JOE SULLIVAN

The pianist Joe Sullivan,
jamming sound against idea

hard as it can go
florid and dangerous

slams at the beat, or hovers,
drumming, along its spikes;

in his time almost the only
one of them to ignore

the chance of easing down,
walking it leisurely,

he'll strut, with gambling shapes,
underpinning by James P.,

amble, and stride over
gulfs of his own leaving, perilously

toppling octaves down to where
the chords grow fat again

and ride hard-edged, most lucidly
voiced, and in good inversions even when

the piano seems at risk of being
hammered the next second into scrap.

For all that, he won't swing
like all the others;

disregards mere continuity,
the snakecharming business,

the 'masturbator's rhythm'
under the long variations:

Sullivan can gut a sequence
in one chorus –

– approach, development, climax, discard –
and sound magnanimous.

The mannerism of intensity
often with him seems true,

too much to be said, the mood
pressing in right at the start, then

running among stock forms
that could play themselves

and moving there with such
quickness of intellect

that shapes flaw and fuse,
altering without much sign,

concentration
so wrapped up in thoroughness

it can sound bluff, bustling,
just big-handed stuff –

belied by what drives him in
to make rigid, display,

shout and abscond, rather
than just let it come, let it go –

And that thing is his mood
a feeling violent and ordinary

that runs in among standard forms so
wrapped up in clarity

that fingers following his
through figures that sound obvious

find corners everywhere,
marks of invention, wakefulness;

the rapid and perverse
tracks that ordinary feelings

make when they get driven
hard enough against time.

Roy Fisher

THE HOME PIANIST'S COMPANION

Clanging along in A-flat
correcting faults,

minding the fifths
and fourths in both hands
and for once
letting the tenths look out
for their own chances,

thinking of Mary Lou,
a lesson to us all,

how she will trench and
trench into the firmness of the music
modestly;

thinking,
in my disorder of twofold sense,
or finding rather
an order thinking for me as I play,
of the look of lean-spoked
railway wagon wheels
clanging on a girder bridge,
chopping the daylight, black
wheel across wheel, spoke

over rim, in behind girder and out
revealing the light, withholding it,
inexorable flickers
of segments in overlap
moving in mean elongate
proportions, the consecutive
fourths of appearances,
harsh gaps, small strong
leverages, never still.

The sour face
on that kind of wheel:
I've known that
ever since I first knew anything;
a primary fact of feeling,
of knowing how
best to look after yourself.

Clanging along in A-flat, and
here they come,
the apports, the arrivals:
fourths, wheel-spokes,
and rapidly the eternal
mask of a narrow-faced cat,
its cornered, cringing intensity
moving me to distraction again.

But into the calm
of a time just after infancy
when most things were still
acceptable

this backward image-trail
projects further
on a straight alignment
across what looked to be emptiness,
checked as void

and suddenly locates the dead,
the utterly forgotten:
primal figure of the line,
primitively remembered,
just a posture of her, an apron,
a gait. Vestigial figure,
neighbouring old woman,
gaunt, narrow-faced, closed in,
acceptable,
soon dead.

Still in the air
haunting the fourths
of A-flat major
with wheels and a glinting cat-face;

reminding me
what it was like to be sure,
before language ever
taught me they were different,
of how some things were the same.

Roy Fisher

ELEGY FOR THELONIOUS

No doctor has put his finger on what is wrong with him, and he has had every medical test under the sun. He's not unhappy, and his mind works very well. He's withdrawn, that's all.
Baroness Pannonica de Koenigswarter

... like your sister trying over sheet music from Woolworth's ...
Philip Larkin

I went to *Jazz on a Summer's Day*
Just to see Thelonious play
His one number — *Blue Monk* — but
As soon as he started his solo they cut
To a yacht race out in the bay.

Rich college kids easy on ear and eye
Unlike dissonant, vinegary
Monk's halting notes, spikey chords, broken runs.
Weird city — but it stuns.
You wonder what's driving the guy.

There has to be something, this is the catch.
No torrent of notes, no technique, can match
The obsessive insistent way
Of a man with things to say
Grimly fighting his demons' clutch.

Sad defeat in the mansion of Nica de K
Ten years a recluse, piano twenty feet away
Untouched — abandoned for bed and the telly
His Nellie (of *Crépescule with Nellie*)
Coming from Harlem to cook every day.

The Man I love, Misterioso, Sweet 'n' Lovely, Monk's Dream
— The best place to listen and brood is at home.
Sweet melodies parodied, wonderingly bent.
He longs to believe in the sweetness — but can't.
Odd pauses — then more tart notes come.

Michael Foley

THE MUSIC OF TIME

Time, said Hawking, runs backwards and is personal. But who didn't know that? Tomorrow's a grey null while forty five years ago is increasingly bright ... and my just-for-you clock makes a seminar last an eternity while semesters go by in a flash. The only question is *how to fight back*. Play, as Earl Hines plays *Indian Summer*, a gleeful revenger disrupting time (whose personal touch was to bury him ... *twice*) exclusively on solo piano now (there's no wish, at sixty nine, to collaborate further) ... though that's not the main point. It's to get at the thing *with your bare hands*, caress, jab and slam, tease and hammer chords to answer the grotesquerie of God by means of irony, dissonance, percussive zest, missing-a-stair-in-the-dark pauses, populous runs, upper-register single notes carefully inset like precious stones with, underneath all that, the rolling bass of squandered years, shame and regret: could have... *should have*... if...if... if... if... back... back... back... back...

Michael Foley

BECHET'S LOW NOTES

A boxer's shuffle
in the resin tray
before he climbs
into the ring
amber grains
beads of gloss
ground into
the foothold
he floats on

or a wall
he presses against
as he plays
the sledge
of each voice
through the dark
of a Texas jail
as they drive
their blues down

or a call
on the reed
              so deep
the groundswell

of the wood
of the African
blackwood
answers more than
he could ask

Roger Garfitt

BIX'S SOLO ON *SINGING THE BLUES*

A sandpiper's call
turning roofline
to shoreline

cornices
to the edge
of a quay

a mooring
on the estuary
of air

where a pigeon
skims itself
like a stone

and flocks of
egrets fold
into magnolias

as if time
had blossomed,
all the time

in the world
before the trumpet
rasps

and he struts
up the avenue
he's just blown away

cock-a-doodle-dandy

Roger Garfitt

SPRING IS HERE
(to the sound of Ben Webster)

First the touch
of the brushes

glistenings
and tricklings
of water under ice

then the south wind
of the bass

the small rain
of the piano...

Warm air ruffles
around a reed

and you unfurl
a scarf

unbutton a long glove
of midnight blue

shimmy and shrug off
a shoulder strap

gleam and escape me

full-bodied flower
on a single stalk
of breath

smoky rose

Roger Garfitt

MINGUS: *SELF-PORTRAIT IN THREE COLOURS*

Not that he glances out of it, he is glancing away,
even the colours are glanced away, doubt overlays them
so that they are fired and burn back through the glaze,

anemones on a café table, arranged in a liturgy of love,
all the colours of blood against the small check of the cloth,
the blue has a premonition, there is an inkling in the red,

but the magentas pulse as they darken, still in flood,
searches rather than colours, chances of the light
as it runs the length of its wave, split seconds that give

the only glimpse of him.

Roger Garfitt

THE CAKEWALK

In smoky limelight of a Smyrna café
He sees them, seven solemn negroes dancing
With faces rapt and out-thrust bellies prancing
In a slow, solemn, ceremonial cakewalk,
Dancing and prancing to the sombre tom-tom
Thumped by a crook-backed grizzled negro squatting.
And as he watches . . . in the steamy twilight
Of a swampy forest in rank greenness rotting,
That sombre tom-tom at his heartstrings strumming
Sets all his sinews twitching and a singing

Of cold fire through his blood — and he is dancing
Among his fellows in the dank green twilight,
With naked, oiled, bronze-gleaming bodies swinging
In a rapt, holy, everlasting cakewalk,
For evermore in slow procession prancing.

Wilfrid Gibson

RAGTIME

A minx in khaki struts the limelit boards:
With false moustache, set smirk, and ogling eyes
And straddling legs and swinging hips she tries
To swagger it like a soldier, while the chords
Of rampant ragtime jangle, clash and clatter,
And over the brassy blare and drumming din
She strains to squirt her squeaky notes and thin
Spirtle of sniggering lascivious patter.

Then out into the jostling Strand I turn,
And down a dark lane to the quiet river,
One stream of silver under the full moon,
And think of how cold searchlights flare and burn
Over dank trenches where men crouch and shiver,
Humming, to keep their hearts up, that same tune.

Wilfrid Gibson

Two curios. "The Cakewalk" seems to have been first published in Edward Marsh's anthology of GEORGIAN POETRY, 1918–19. In Gibson's large COLLECTED POEMS 1905–1925, it appears in a section called "In Khaki", while "The Cakewalk" is the second poem in the section that follows, called "Travels".

MR. ACKER BILK

The snazzy silk waistcoats are gaudy as deckchairs
set fluttering all the way along the striped sand
as the New Hippodrome management proudly presents
Mr. Acker Bilk and his Paramount Jazz Band

— on whose sleeve notes Teutonic upper case Incipits
augment a diction that's pure Brobdingnag aureate:
Herein the Ensemble's Titular Head executes
Effusions so far Unparalleled upon the Clarionett.

But nothing's distorted tonight as *Tiger Rag*
thumps its way out under the stuccoed awning
of the proscenium, where bright blue birds hover
and the rock solid cliffs of Dover will hit morning

into a cocked hat, a bowler hat, or any God
– blessed hat that you like, up as high as your top C;
in the meantime, *Let it shine — o good Lord let it shine,*
let the light from that lighthouse shine on me!

Now into the pit and the stalls ranges his raw blues;
Dardanella, a cold shiver under the sunshades
— the beach is a desolate sidewalk where over-leafed
gangsters sit cautiously sipping iced lemonades.

Time chastens us all, band, gangsters, fat usherettes
wading awkwardly out to sea for the rowdy encore
— which is the Hippodrome Manager, crossing the bar
fifty years hence, still whistling *Stranger on the Shore.*

John Gohorry

CHET BAKER

looks out from his hotel room
across the Amstel to the girl
cycling by the canal who lifts
her hand and waves and when
she smiles he is back in times
when every Hollywood producer
wanted to turn his life
into that bitter-sweet story
where he falls badly, but only
in love with Pier Angeli,
Carol Lynley, Natalie Wood;
that day he strolled into the studio,
fall of fifty-two, and played
those perfect lines across
the chords of *My Funny Valetine* –
and now when he looks up from
his window and her passing smile
into the blue of a perfect sky
he knows this is one of those
rare days when he can truly fly.

John Harvey

GHOST OF A CHANCE

He plays the tune lazily,
pretty much the way he must
have heard Billie sing it,
but slower, thick-toned,
leaning back upon the beat,
his mind half on the melody,
half on the gin.

Between takes he stands,
head down, shrunken inside
a suit already overlarge,
cheeks sunken in.
He thinks of her, Billie:
already it is possible
he has started to bleed within.

From the control room, laughter,
but that's not the sound he hears;
tenor closer to his mouth,
he turns towards the doors:
unseen, not quite unbidden,
someone has just slipped in.

At the end of eight bars
he closes his eyes and blows.
After two choruses he will cover
his mouthpiece with its shield:
not play again.

John Harvey

BAND CALL

Horn	You are a snarly broth and breath of a lion with its eye-teeth in the sun's shoulder, cut loose, riding its golden high; then loping off in a cool pride of violence deferred.
Drums	You are woodpeckers drilling a dream forest, a million reindeer running with the wind, a rogue elephant crashing through leaves of moonlight, a gorilla with a deep chestful of anger battering hairy defiance.

Sax You are a shifty shambly furry bear,
a slouchy smoochy honey of a bear
slowly climbing a hive-set tree;
coming down again slow, drippy,
to earthy, curly sleep.

Clarinet You are a curlew scaling wild summits,
planing down a heavenly trill...
a smoke-tailed squirrel branch dissolved;
a snake swimming suave lagoons...
that melts in mazy grass.

Guitar You are a swan reflecting summer,
a saunter of white birds on downy stretches,
a girl's hand drifting the side of a boat...
a blue note plucked out of the sky, lost
in a river ringing with trout-ripples.

Band You are an elephant jiving rings round a squirrel,
a reindeer crossed with a rainbow trout,
a bear-baiting yaffle, a mad gorilla,
a snake swallowing a muted lion,
a curlew that sings for a girl's white hand

You are jazz

Geoffrey Holloway

IMPROVISATION

Jazz: neither the grip
of perfect unity
nor the lax
unlovely scrimmage.
Trombone, clarinet, sax
like braiding water slip,
the image
of good community.

Richard Kell

TWO JAZZ SONNETS FROM EARLIER YEARS

1

I like the way they drift, not talking much,
in denim jeans and leather, with long hair
flowing across their shoulders, and an air
of dreamy patience, open to the touch
of Pan or Dionysus as they wait
for the last jazz performance to begin.
The matinée's ending now: they listen in,
hunched on the littered grass outside the gate.
Dreamy or bored? Our bodies move, but they,
the devotees, remain as still as wax.
Could be that I mythologised a sad
conformity, insensitive to the play
of drum and clarinet, trombone and sax,
with longing for the youth I never had.

2

Light fades along the river. Quiet ripples
massage the glistening mudbanks at low tide,
and car doors bang on silence. Older here,
late twenties, thirties, letting go to ease
the tension of propriety or fear,
they stroll towards the pub in groups and couples.
The jazz-blast hits them as they step inside.
Then time gives way to tempo: by degress
liquor and music charm divided selves
to know the strange polyphony they are.
Quick fingers fall to stillness on the keys:
that final chord... The watcher at the bar
turns off the coloured lamps along the shelves
and bawls across the room 'Time gentlemen please'.

Richard Kell

ANGEL EYES

The singer is giving us *Angel Eyes*
and already tonight
she has swung us down a long blue trail,
that old jazz canon of love, betrayal
longing and despair.

Thin child, a mystery, how, at her age,
she knows all this so well, but the voice,
high, sweet-sour and breathless,
persuades us as it floats out
on the cellar's husky air.

For the rest of her, why – nothing more
than a rag, this clinging whisper of a dress,
a bone – lying far too near to the skin –
and that gloriously black
and shining hank of hair.

Angela Kirby

THREE SINGERS

Nina Simone at the 'Village Gate'

Face of a brainy,
precocious child –
'The Times are Changing'
'It's the Morning of My Life'
then 'Turning Point' – a very
touching little tale
of a little white girl and her
little black schoolfriend.
last line is 'Oh, I see...'

'I'm Gonna Leave You.'
She has the air
of a princess, a
Benin bronze. Poem by
Paul Laurence Dunbar
as a song, 'Compensation'
('An' if you dunno
who Dunbar was, find out.')
– 'God in his great compassion
gave me the gift of soul...'

The way she turns
while playing and
peers through the spots
at me over her
slight left shoulder,
hunch of a hunch.
'Someone out there,'
she mutters, not
seeing I see her.

'Any Day Now I Shall Be Released.'
No smiles, few words,
scornful; only gesture
a lifting, very occasional,
of right hand and forefinger
Revival revivalism.

'I Ain't Got No One'
(terrific). Sometimes
half-rises to sing a phrase
into the pendant mike
angles over the Steinway
that seems hardly able to believe
her fingers in the solos, her voice in
'I Could Eat a Book.'

'I Put a Spell on You.'

Anita O'Day at 'The Half Note'

Hookey's and the 5-Spot all closed down,
only the Half Note now,
corner Spring and Hudson,
going since 1957, one
of the oldest in the Village.

Roy Eldridge warming up
(he's still wearing his glasses–
he takes them off to get hot).
Plays and sings (yes)
'Have You Ever Loved a Woman?'
'Everything you do is wrong–
like Hong Kong.'
Private fun in the band – Roy's
lovely mischievous grin.
Snub Moseley on slide trombone
'and slide sax.'

It's Anita!
She's really here!
Neat in white lace
(from Bangkok, she told me later,
'Just did a Far East tour there,
and next year Japan – all
those cherry-red plastic pressings.')
She makes all her own dresses, too –
there's a girl for you!

Unbelievable
She asked me what I'd like her
to start with, and naturally
I said 'It Had to be You' – but
she didn't have it ready, so
the pianist used it as an intro as
she waved a kiss to me.

Her first number, for me alone,
'Let Me Off Uptown'.
(Shall I ever forget?)
'Yesterday.'
'Try Your Wings.'
'Do You know the Way to San José?' –
She shreds a lyric like e.e.cummings.

Those little white gloves
caress the mike. She smiles
softly (that cute brown mole
upper lip left of centre),
waves at my strobe flash,
'They Can't Take That Away From Me.'
'Let's Fall in Love'.
I'm not going to cry any more –
'Let Someone Start Believing in You –
Watch what happens...'

She signs a record even she
has forgotten, it's so rare,
it makes her give a little frown –
EP Norgran 'Anita Sings' and she writes
'To James – and one of his most
treasured possessions – from
Anita O'Day'.

Next set.
She says, 'Change the pace a little bit' –
Her favourite phrase.
And mine.

Fats Waller

On his pink velvet tabouret
at the honkytonk upright
bouncing
beat to the bar
the plump thighs
in tight pants
the tiny feet
pumping the pedals
the sideways grin
beneath the tilted
derby
the ten little fingers
twinkling in the keys
like fat fish
gold-ringed
in a black-and-white bet
the scratched warmth
of that voice –

'Ooh-ooh!
You gave me a load of
squirrel-juice –
you got me
runnin' up a tree...'

Me too.

James Kirkup

JAZZBO LE GRIOT POEM

Jazzbo Le Griot was a bebop drummer,
hot like sunlight in the summer.
Jazzbo went to college to obtain some knowledge.
and had to dig and delve, rummage and forage.
An urbane dude, never rude refined not crude,
he found his sojourn through the world of "what its supposed
to be",
between you and me,
a very straight-jackets-ville kinda episode.
Cos all the college dudes ever played was arpeggios, chords,
runs and scales.
But to Jazzbo a saxophone was a thing that wailed with the
spirit of an
ancestrally guided creativity, soul on ice pure spontaneity.
It spoke of the liberation from a life time of those coal black
blues. But to the college dudes this was Jazzbo being rude.
He said,
"Wohohoho! wohohoho! woh Jazzbo LeGriot! Wohohoho!
wohohoho! He played it with that feel, Wohohoho!
wohohoho! Jazzbo's jazz was real".

He realised that Jazz had been kidnapped before his eyes,
captured, disconnected, controlled and infected with a sterile
style, similar to that of a dry martini or a cocktail inbetweeny
wearing a wry dinner jacket smile, not so much a lounge lizard,
more of a lounge crocodile.
"It's all about chords & scales & things said the college buffs, as
they did their stuff running up and down scales, arpeggios and
things,
they were running up and down stairs, corridors, everywhere
looking for the Jazz that really kicked ass.
But academia had taken Jazz to the clinic and committed a
most uncool crime, by actually leaving Jazz smack dab in it.

Confined to the cold grey squares in a jazzy check jacket,
jazz had become reduced to what was loosely referred to as a classic.
Jazzbo said, "I thought it was a good idea to translate 'Opera' from Italian into English, at least now we can understand what it is that's been boring us for all these years".
He was joking but the dude was almost in tears, to think that the sound that these clowns were putting down once upon a time was more than a stultified fad:
now it was background music at the mad hatters tea party where everything good was bad.
Glorious jazz rooted in, and born out of the black people,
trying to do their own thing, as independent equals,
once joyful, playful and wantonly wicked in its natural innocence,
breaking down barriers in a society segregated situation and cleansing the air like incense.
Born from the goodnews of gospel-blues,
and a heartical non partial orchestration.
A collective groove with a liberated dude riffing on a cue, till his individual voice comes through, so that he can enthusiastically say his piece,
tongue moving in rhythm in time to the beat.
Yea! The jazz Jazzbo knew was the jazz that had wings, a sound that's only heard when someones soul sings.
He popped his head into the rehearsal room, and added a light note to the arrangement of things by saying,
"Yo! dudes this may sound to you's like new news and you might not even like my views,
but jazz aint scales and chords and arpeggios and things, you see jazz is from the soul that's why
JAZZ SWINGS...
this aint a thing to do with black & white, it's more to do with attitude and how you feel inside, Jazzbo went to the college to get some lessons, ended up giving one, that may have made the wrong impression, cos all the intellectuals thought that he was messing when he yelled, "Yo! Society this is a Jam session.

Wohohoho! wohohoho! woho Jazzbo LeGriot! Wohohoho!
wohohoho! He played it with that feel! Wohohoho!
wohohoho! He played Jazz for real.
Jazzbo.

MKE Lange

FOR SIDNEY BECHET

That note you hold, narrowing and rising, shakes
Like New Orleans reflected on the water,
And in all ears appropriate falsehood wakes,

Building for some a legendary Quarter
Of balconies, flower-baskets and quadrilles,
Everyone making love and going shares—

Oh, play that thing! Mute glorious Storyvilles
Others may license, grouping round their chairs
Sporting-house girls like circus tigers (priced

Far above rubies) to pretend their fads,
While scholars *manqués* nod around unnoticed
Wrapped up in personnels like old plaids.

On me your voice falls as they say love should,
Like an enormous yes, My Crescent City
Is where your speech alone is understood,

And greeted as the natural noise of good,
Scattering long-haired grief and scored pity.

Philip Larkin

SECOND TROMBONE

Maybe somewhere you can still be heard,
on airshots from abandoned stations,
or on the cracked shellac,
an extra voice, fleshing out harmonies
under the scuffling surface:
music made some ancient afternoon
for an impresario who never paid you.

Otherwise, only this photograph,
jaggedly creased: a mass of scatchy lines
barely concealing you from recognition.

On the bass-drum a name
ornately lettered,
grandiloquently obscure.

Richard Leigh

FOR JOHN STEVENS

After a well-meant eulogy
which tries to be specific
but almost reduces you
to everybody's virtures

and after you've been rendered down
to a handful of ashes and bonedust,
it is finally time to drink –
your local, a closed world
of noise, and smoke,
and booze, and awkward humour.

'til chucking-out time
it hasn't really happened:

this is a gig, no more. And you?
Stuck in the traffic somewhere,
cursing God and man.

Out in the night, though, the truth
makes itself known to us:
you have been indispensable,
but now we must learn to manage.

Funeral-rites are the start
of a slow letting-go.

Memory is salvage, or invention –

And bereavement, a powerless fury.

Richard Leigh

DOCTOR JAZZ

Hello, Central! Give me Doctor Jazz!

Jelly Roll Morton

To be nearly as great as you
Think you are, play the same tunes
Again and again: small fortunes,
Diamonds for each hollow tooth.

Django Reinhardt

A whole new method compensates
For your damaged fingers: sweat
In the creases of your forehead,
Mother-of-pearl between the frets.

King Oliver

Now all pretenders to the throne
Learn how the patient gums decay,
Music hurts: though they took away
Your bad breath, the crown's your own.

Billie Holiday

You fastened to your bony thigh
Some dollar bills and waited for
The cacophonous janitor
And silence and the cue to die.

Michael Longley

WORDS FOR JAZZ PERHAPS

for Solly Lipsitz

Elegy for Fats Waller

Lighting up, lest all our hearts should break,
His fiftieth cigarette of the day,
Happy with so many notes at his beck
And call, he sits there taking it away,
The maker of immaculate slapstick.

With music and with such precise rampage
Across the deserts of the blues a trail
He blazes, towards the one true mirage,
Enormous on a nimble-footed camel
And almost refusing to be his age.

He plays for hours on end and though there be
Oases one part water, two parts gin,
He tumbles past to reign, wise and thirsty,
At the still centre of his loud dominion—
THE SHOOK THE SHAKE THE SHEIKH OF ARABY.

Bud Freeman in Belfast

Fog horn and factory siren intercept
Each fragile hoarded-up refrain. What else
Is there to do but let those notes erupt

Until your fading last glissando settles
Among all other sounds — carefully wrapped
In the cotton wool from aspirin bottles?

To Bessie Smith

You bring from Chattanooga Tennessee
Your huge voice to the back of my mind
Where, like sea shells salvaged from the sea
As bright reminders of a few weeks' stay,
Some random notes are all I ever find.
I couldn't play your records every day.

I think of Tra-na-rossan, Inisheer,
Of Harris drenched by horizontal rain–
Those landscapes I must visit year by year.
I do not live with sounds so seasonal
Nor set up house for good. Your blues contain
Each longed-for holiday, each terminal.

To Bix Beiderbecke

In hotel rooms, in digs you went to school.
These dead were voices from the floor below
Who filled like an empty room your skull,

Who shared your perpetual one-night stand
—The havoc there, and the manoeuvrings!—
Each coloured hero with his instrument.

You were bound with one original theme
To compose in your head your terminus,
Or to improvise with the best of them

That parabola from blues to barrelhouse.

Michael Longley

JUG BAND
in memory of Philip Larkin

We would follow that New Orleans marching band
As it passes the settee for the hundredth time,
But we have left clarinet and drums behind
And make up the instuments, and then the theme,

And the theme is the making up of instruments,
Jugs and kazoos for us to improvise our souls,
Thimbles for keeping time with and making sense
On a washboard of our uncomplicated roles.

Michael Longley

TALES FROM THE (ENGLISH) JAZZ AGE
for Jim Burns

Spud Murphy, Preston's first known jazzman,
stood by his feisty, green-stockinged wife
in your dad's good-for-men-only local

ordering pints to a jaw-clenched
silent riff of "Poof, weirdo,

Red." Your tale, Jim, but how about
Birmingham '52 and GO HOME DIRTY BOPPER,
that hooray banner slung against Bruce Turner
when Lyttleton's band played City Hall

and found no place to eat after the show.
Still, it *was* 10 pm and Jim – remember? –,
Humph's own 100 Club licensed *soft drinks only*,

There, I first heard Broonzy's
tar-and-bourbon voice, heard more recently how,
delivered standard-fare for his Nottingham gig,

the owner of a chintz-infested hotel
came out to greet Big Bill with
"No coloureds, I've got my name to think of."

Or Mansfield, "Sin City of the Midlands".
With Ken Colyer due, of course
the local jazz club's plea

for a late bar had no joy, though as
old growly bear told it,
"we stomped the night away

until the wee small hour of 10.30pm"
"Joyless" the O.E.D. says:
"having or causing neither joy nor pleasure".

Jim, in my lexicon,
joyless means that heart-in-splints
bollock-brain state you scorn:

joyless means jazzless, right?

John Lucas

STROLLING

in blue shades
summer saunters in
                                        Hi man

it's Ben taking a break

he wants to let me know
swing's small combo come-back
is blue skies overdue

like post-winter loving
that laze of limbs before down-
stairs eggs spread
across hot virgin oil —
panscape of cirrostratus
with lambent sun
                                        soft

radiance Ben breathes
a mellowind that flitters
easy-over warmth
                                        well
stroll on Ben stroll on

John Lucas

FATS AT THE BBC, 1938

"Is y'all on Fats?" he challenged his vast bum,
and span round on the Corporation's stool.
Forever misbehaving, he'd become
very good friends with English jazzmen, "cool"

wasn't in vogue and soon the good times rolled:
coaxed by his fingers *Honeysuckle Rose*
showered the stuffy air with summer gold
as a wintry Oxbridge voice announced him. "Those

Happy Harlem Days with Mr Waller
and – His Rhythm." "Mercy me" Fats shouted,
"Now listen up, this here ain't no dam' scholar:
jes' call me Fats until I'm good and dead."

Death soon got him down. He was on a train
going nowhere much when the cold stilled his voice.
But no, I pile all of him on again
and again, he spins, Fats lives, and I rejoice.

John Lucas

CUTTING A RUG

cut a rug: To 'jive' or 'jitterbug': dance addicts: adopted from US soldiers in 1943.
ERIC PARTRIDGE: *A Dictionary of Slang* (1982 edn.)

Was it some kind of record? My first day
at boarding school, aged eight, taught me a thing
or two about authority, the church,
justice and so on, but you don't complain
about the status quo – you're stuck with that.
I knew how homesick, foreign, oddly named

and scared I was: you simply scowled, the pain
was nothing you'd admit. But why should I
have done the surreal deed of which I stood
accused? Unthinkable! Sheer pointlessness
denying crime … My protests did no good
under the circumstances: I'd been framed
and never in my schooldays found out why.

Horribly flexible, the slippers used
for beating boasted half-inch rubber soles.
You bent bare-bottomed by the bed while he,
Headmaster Reverend Aubrey Hooper, swung
hard, wholly unerring as to aim, and
skillfully apt to make small buttocks sting.
My situtation as I saw it then –
undignified, odd, laughable, unfair –
might not have altered radically with time:
you get to know the score. To take a pair
of scissors and deliberately destroy
the fringe of Jackson Major's blanket, well,
sinful behaviour's punished in a boy,
six strokes for that. Prep school did not prepare
me to deal so promptly with the absurd,
fierce eccentricities of life, though Hell
was one daft notion I still turned down flat.

A taste of injustice and all that jazz?
I could laugh the day after, when the word
went round a disbelieving school how I
was beaten for a novel crime, *cutting a rug.*
Can you beat that? They couldn't. I'd enjoy
friends, games, orthodox lessons (more or less),
hot summer days that cannot burn again.
Everyone wondered why I'd vandalize
an older boy's bedding. The pattern's clear
enough, memory folds a bluegreen tartan
into place, pristine, intact and neat as

myself then. Holding fast under duress,
a hedonist Greek I feigned being Spartan
until my time was right, when to cut loose
was paradise.
                    I laughed for real, amused
that words would never leave me in the lurch.
Language and jazz and women – my loves fused,
suggesting via that Ellingtonian's band
how jovial pleasure, art, time's subtle beat
could all meet and endure forty years on:
Cootie Williams & His Rug Cutters. They
play – and for the record I am grateful, gone.

Alexis Lykiard

THE JAM MAN

As a
jazzer
Gaillard, Slim
was far more fun than dismal Jim
Witherspoon. He
invented Vout-o-roonee
cheered up bop and made us laugh.
Smiles pre-empt his epitaph.

One of a kind, whom nothing could faze.
Slim liked to cook, wore white berets.
Now, if anyone can, he'll soon inveigle
The Powers That Be to dunk a bagel.

Alexis Lykiard

THE CHORD'S RARE
(overheard on a band bus)

Art Farmer who dug Bill Evans,
Harold Land by thy name.
Thy swing has come,
Thy Teddy Bunn,
on *Birth of the Blues* as on *Blue Seven.*

Give us this Lady Day our daily Bird
And *Four Brothers* our Tristanos,
Aretha give them that trade fours against us
And lead us hot into Hawes, Hampton
But deliver us from Devo.

George Wein is the swingdom, Bud Powell and Med Flory,
For Elvin and Elvin, Coltrane

Alexis Lykiard

AVOGADRO'S NUMBER

Lick the doughnut sugar from your fingers
Memories stir (Proust was here)
Winter
The houses all huddled up together
trying to keep warm.
In a yellow pool of light
his fingers swarmed over the double bass
like an octopus on a railway track
keep up now keep up

Embraceable you, she sang
the rain hissed on the long black road
liquorice for the cars to eat
Sweet street.

He packed himself in a leather jacket
(Pink soft nipples)
and went out into the fog

The air came close
Breath was like a white flag

Soon home

Sue May

FLUGEL
for Dick Pearce

What happened to the flugelhorn
you always played, that had you
turn down trumpet gigs, the famous
brother too brash, too much
like the army that could not
sustain itself on minor modal scales?

Did you buy yourself out, grow
your hair, practise, practise, find
the melting, mellow sound of
private life less trumpet loud, play
the fatter horn, because it caught
a quieter, self-effacing mood?

You were never one for soaring
high, preferring Miles to Dizzy
any day, Rollins to Bird. Is it
because bewildered in a world
you can't believe you helped create,
you must speak louder now?

So many lack technique, can only
marvel at a winged horn that puffs
the air with proof that gentle rain
can slake a giant thirst. Did it grow
too comfortable, so much the salve
you locked away its charm for good?

As if suddenly you were a sophist
duping those who'll follow any lure
that takes them out beyond the boom
of modern gods towards the human
birdsong that's heartsease if only
temporarily, then temporarily at least.

Paul McLoughlin

AFRICAN NEGATIVES

for Alan Ross

The Best of Mobley's in the entrance hall,
with Paul Gonzalves, Oscar's *Night Train*,
Ernie Wilkins, hardback histories and more
– America second-hand and trestled,
the poems of Maya Angelou something new.

Out in the bar there's live jazz keen ears
can hear under the soundtrack's lush swell
for another Oscar, Wilde, half-hidden
by a colonnade, Bosie arriving
in a swoop of luggage: Paris on the turn.

The spine of Ross's book leaps out,
is mine for a back-pocket fiver, was

ten and six when it came out, old dosh.
I wave aside the 5p change to flick
the peach pages of a lover's find.

The black manager is searching through
a weight of keys, unlocks the cinema,
smiles only when she sees the wallet
lodged between our back-row seats –
library cards for Cambridge, London,

Manchester, Leeds. Plastic sesames
to Rare Reading Rooms! Then home,
a beer and Kenny Garrett's alto
on an eighteen quid CD. I know my jazz,
have most of what they had for sale.

Julian Joseph overflowed his stool,
found a sudden Latin groove in octaves
with the resident guitarist lost. He
was older, wider than I'd thought, perched
like that wiry Blue Note cover sketch

of Horace Silver on *Blowin' the Blues*
Away – not, as I could have sworn,
Song for My Father, probably because
my dad forgot things, too, without having to
to love, like Ross's couple in Bloemfontein:

He not quite white
As she, nor she
So black as he. It wasn't
a terminal complaint,
more like a matter of degree.

Paul McLoughlin

LISTEN HERE

While the opening credits of *Last Tango* rolled,
I whispered this was Gato Barbieri, later that the arranger
must be Oliver Nelson.

I did it again when I heard Billy Joel's
Just The Way You Are. That alto solo
had to be Phil Woods'.

The point is not that I'm insufferable,
but that they're recognizable a few bars in,
from anywhere.

Paul McLoughlin

JESS STACY

He owned that kind of lyrical command
That was so much admired. These were the days
Of piano culture in America.
Stacy sat easy, gathered in long-fingered hands
Octaves and basses, and never turned a phrase
That did not evoke some helpless metaphor
Of something crystalline or something clean,
Abstracted but committed, intense and yet serene.
In Goodman's band he was like a hidden spring
In constant flow. Alone, his lines would swing
Lightly, with a deft sustaining tremor. Often enough
It was among the bold brass necks and the tough
Chicago swagger that he placed his clarity:
Silencing a barroom with a line of poetry.

Peter McSloy

ART PEPPER

A damned uncompromising type was Art:
There was the early hard-nosed vanity,
In never running with the Parker pack,
In saturnine good looks, in being smart
The way a hustler has the need to be.
Then, bearing the weight of all this on his back,
Inventing a style that spoke of such a life,
Alert, short-winded, stabbing like a knife.
At last the prison-pale, crop-haired survivor,
With eyes that had seen it all, and still intent
On his choice of ways to drive himself to hell.
The night when he and Stitt allowed no favor,
But each played everything he knew, this meant
Far more than health, than life, this thing he could do well.

Peter McSloy

FREDDIE GREEN

Time, time. Engine-beat, cat's tread.
Machine that breathes, a bouncing ball, a throb.
Harmonic pulse, knife-edge of walking bass,
Each stroke precisely laid in space,
Moving through slight manipulations of the chord,
For forty years and more, as Schuller said,
A quarter billion beats, he did his job,
He worked his strip of ground, the finger-board.
Rhythm guitar. A craft no-one aspires
To live or die for, too much like lighting fires
In other people's houses. Some of us, though,
By work at small perfections come to know
Great structures rest on every single point.
And the time, the time, was never out of joint.

Peter McSloy

THE HARD BLUES

Listening to Julius Hemphill's
Theatrical, soaring *Roi Boye*
Mourning his loss
Whilst reading about Emmett Till

Julius's chilly sibilance
Bearing witness

Transported to Mississippi's echo chamber

Three months before Emmett was killed
The Reverend George Lee, from Belzoni
(Delta town – spawning Pinetop Perkins
And Eddie "Guitar" Burns)
Shot dead
A traffic accident
The authorites said
"Lee the first Black
To register to vote
In the county"
(Suggested sound track to these lines:
Max Roach's 'Mendacity',
Or J.B. Lenoir's 'Down in Mississippi',
"Open season" deplored
And, on other tracks from the same LP,
Imploring Presidents to act)

Back to *The Hard Blues*
Of Julius
And other Hemphills down there
(Salient but unrelated)

In Como
The She-Wolf
Jessie Mae

Playing her Diddley Bow
Potent art and history
Drumming with grandfather Sidney
In fife and fiddle bands
Lonnie Pitchford   riches galore
On other ancient instruments
And the piano's sustain reverberates
Gospel
In an ice storm
Life threatening
Sustained by song

And I can remember listening to
Satoka Fujii and Natsuki Tamura's
How Many?
And Albert Ayler
Live in Greenwich Village
In storms
Deluge
Electric

The Delta
Southern sediment

A poisoned southern well.

Stephen C. Middleton

CYPRESS GROVE

… and Bertha Lee sliced
    Charley's throat, they say
(Bukka thought he died that way)
The wellspring almost dry

An icy chill brings Honeyboy
Running to the graveside
(Like Ishman Bracey "fell down on (his) knees")
Missing posterity
On the move
Riding the blind

It's one step removed, again –
Patton, Robert Johnson –
From the treasure trove

(Hard times)
White whiskey/no money
In the Depression
Later a Hobo Jungle downfall
For hoarse voiced Tommy McClennan

And Big Joe
So cantankerous
That he missed death
In a car with Peetie Wheatstraw
(The Devil's Son in Law)
By a whisper

And Hambone Willie Newbern
Killed in prison (says Sleepy John)

Frail American dreams
The Delta horizon
And some lonely Cypress Grove.

Stephen C. Middleton

GOODBYE

He breathed in air, he breathed out light.
Charlie Parker was my delight.

Adrian Mitchell

JIMMY GIUFFRE PLAYS 'THE EASY WAY'

A man plodding through blue-grass fields.
He's here to decide whether the grass needs mowing.
He sits on a mound and taps his feet on the deep earth.
He decides the grass doesn't need mowing for a while.

Adrian Mitchell

BUDDY BOLDEN

He bust through New Orleans
On his cornet night and day,
Buddy kept on stompin'
Till he was put away.

He chose his girls like kings do
And drank like earth was hell,
But when they tried to cut him
He played like Gabriel.

The notes shot out his cornet
Like gobs come off a ship.
You felt the air get tighter
And then you heard it rip.

They threw him in the bughouse
And took away his horn.
He hadn't felt so mean since
The day that he was born.

Some say corn liquor done it
Or layin' a bad whore
But I guess he blew so much out
He couldn't think no more.

Adrian Mitchell

DEEP PURPLE WINE

Friday in a city
    That was growling with the heat
I saw the tall rain coming
    Walking with a steady beat
It walked right down the sky
    And then scuttled off down the street

Seven in the evening
    Yellow streetlights start to shine
I turned to my woman
    She locked her eyes on mine
She said: Best thing when it's raining
    Is a bottle of Deep Purple Wine

It makes your spirit laugh
    It makes your spirit moan
It makes you feel you're talking to
    An angel on the phone
It cools you then it fools you
    And it warms you to the bone

Duke Ellington invented it
    The greatest ever brew
It was made by Jimmy Blanton
    And by Johnny Hodges too
And it was gurgled out with every note
    Old Cootie Williams blew

It tickles like the old pianner
    Mrs Klinkscale taught
It's heavy as the drum-kit
    That Louis Bellson fought
It's light and bright as a kitten
    Or a Billy Strayhorn thought

Tricky Sam Nanton
    Poured it into crazy shapes
Cat Anderson employed it
    In miraculous escapes
Sonny Greer Ray Nance Rex Stewart
    They were all vintage grapes

Don't forget Ben Webster
    Barney Bigard Lawrence Brown
They filled a big cloud with that wine
    And sailed it over town
And every night in Ellington
    That wine came pouring down

Such Sweet Thunder in the throat
    Such a Crescendo In Blue
Black Brown and Beige jump out your cage
    And start Slappin' Seventh Avenue
It Don't Mean A Thing If It Ain't Got That Swing
    Like East St Louis Toodle-oo

So drink to the great Duke Ellington
    And the Deep Purple Wine he made
Deep Purple Wine gives you dancing feet
    Like kangaroos on parade
Deep Purple Wine so fine so fine
    It will never ever fade

Thanks, Duke.

Adrian Mitchell

LISTENING

… each ear
Is listening to its hearing, so none hear.
W. H. Auden

So you play a little, you said. *Well*
Listen to this – Ben Webster's
Tenor, Oscar Peterson, and both of us
Unwinding after yet another
Local reading you'd arranged –
Sheer Poetry! If we'd played them this …
Ah yes, if we'd played them this –
Already we were old conspirators –
I smiled back at you, squinting
Through a murky tumbler, your propitiatory
Double-scotch for guests – *I'm sorry,*
Really, about the numbers. They'd probably have been
The same if you were famous. Or even, of course,
If we had played them this …

It's the way he breathes. You can hear it.
I could, but then you watched me
Hearing it, you watched
Merely for confirmation just as earlier
You'd heard me read, not hearing
What I had written …

Listen, though, you insisted
Can you describe it? There isn't a word.
No, there wasn't, not then
With you expecting it and me
The Visiting Poet, but last night
After nine years I heard the track again
And suddenly I was squinting at you
Through that tumbler, smiling
As I wrote down this … I heard
The fugitive gift of tongues,

A halo of resonant air
Around the mouthpiece, the invisible
Rhythms pulsing out and out
Towards containment, each
Note a mere particular, the quick
Melodic husk already
Cracked into silence, a freedom beyond wings ...

Yes, but listen, you say, *all those words, words,*
And you still don't hear it
Even the breath swings.

John Mole

BENNY GOODMAN

Studying the dance-floor
Through a scholar's glasses,
Soul of strict measure
And precise notation –

Running wild,
His cool quicksilver
Head arrangements
Darted into place,

Or flying home
In a white tuxedo
With the boys behind him
And the heat turned on

He came and conquered,
Little Caesar,
Colonising jazz
From town to town

And so to Moscow
Where the iron curtain
Rose for him
Although *With Benny*

Every gig (a sideman said)
Was like playing in Russia,
Swing on the rocks,
A counterpoint of ice.

John Mole

WILD BILL

Not for him, the tremulous
vibrato of age, lip gone
or the bought-in teeth
on an instalment plan.
This is the furious
Fuck you, death
in the full face of it.
This is my man.

Wild Bill, all in his name
he stands here, hot
and ready. One by one
the boys step up
to claim their solo spot,
rehearsed, well-amplified.
A brisk shrug
as they move aside.

At last, the triple-fingered
loosening of valves,
arms up and out, he
glares at the microphone,

twists it the other way
then with a flat-
down stamp of his foot
begins to play.

John Mole

A SIGNALMAN HEARS JAZZ

The signal-box stands on its timber cradle
Beside the running tracks of steel;
Travellers passing see a chrysalis of light,
A man hunched motionless within.

Darkness;
Signal lights flame red and green,
His hand heaves a lever and points shift,
Directing the hurtling tons of iron.

But what they cannot see surrounds him,
Unfolding wings of sound:
Saxophones, trumpets, drums beating
In tumult – a Kansas City chorus
That insentient freight deafens
Then fades back into his space in night.

Gripping the lever, he stares as they pass,
Trains that carried roosting bluesmen
From the delta to Chicago, New York,
Shake his still reflection.

He drags back his hand,
Dreams out the scream of metals,
His ear searching this crucible
For the frail chords.

A freighter passes, its brake locked on a wheel,
Pouring sparks furiously onto the chippings;
He leaps up at the molten glow of steel,
Pressing his cupped hands to the glass
Where his eye and imagination fuse –

The fire in the night,
Note after note spilling in him.

Graham Mort

JAZZ

It is to you, my dear, I owe
This love of the soloing saxophone.
You are going away, for a while.
I have borne that before.
I am only afraid
Of the highly-strung bass
Like a clock in the groin.

Sean O'Brien

ON THE LINE

Close night, and wine.
Forties' jazz in the dark.
A lamp made by me
solid, and suiting the table
bird-wings fluted and slender.

My fingers
dance to the music.
I hear Billie Holiday –
she sounds youthful
fresh from flight.

But I smell the old oils
a senescence in the air.
Her past life was cold
internal wars become bitter.
Now she surprises me

to find my embarrassed tone
as if she knew I was alone
an insomniac visualising her closeness
mixing colour
kneading her out of others.

A half-remembered promise
stubborn, and clinging
is returning in my life
like the song around a rim
made by a finger on glass.

William Park

BLUE LOU

The tops of the poplars sway,
dark horizons, or a score
of horizons?
I imagine Wardell Gray
swaying, as he rendered
Blue Lou.
Rain, another evening
rain.

William Park

JAZZ TRAIN

Empty now but for the band
    it makes its way past platforms
left deserted in the rain –
    through tunnels, sidings, cuttings
and lost villages like these
    where all we hear are notes
and undertones; shrill pleadings

from the trumpet
    or the solo saxophone;
the rhythm section going mad,
    a faded vocalist who swings
with one white orchid
pinned behind her ear.
Pale ghosts climb down

from pit-heads and applaud.
    The passengers have left them,
gone back home, remembering
    only this and nights
like this. She might wake up
    and take him by the hand;
he might turn over in his sleep.

The band is rattling
    through the haunted towns;
searching for a way to make it start –
    to get between the dreamer
and the dream; a blue note
    humming down the miles of track;
a new republic of the heart.

Ian Parks

EYES FOR YOU

Listen! For me without my glasses on
the man on vibes on the record cover
blurs into merely human, but his imp-
ish improvisation is as clear as a lover
likes the reasons why he's loved … Some chimp-
anzee grunts an answer to Hamp's fili-
gree of notes. *Blue Panassié*'s not blue,
tapping out no reason why. It'd be silly
to expect such swing to stamp an extra shoe
to make its point. Now I'm bespectacled
I can make out the features of this true-
blue American in Paris and his hammers.
Visually he's become himself, receptacled.
But his *I only have eyes for you*'s for you
and struck in divinely resonant stammers.

Christopher Pilling

ART PEPPER TAKES OFF

Art Pepper, grown-up kid,
intrepid
in the choice
and timing of his absence notes.
You can hear his voice –
it comes off the page and floats
convincingly in unlicked pre-adolescence
for his voice hasn't broken,
isn't broken. Once
he's pieced his paragraphs together, it's as if he's spoken
for missing parents, but he's letting
the improvisation speak
for itself, whetting
our lickerish taste-buds, tweak

-ing the mel
-ody in hopes it will gell
for him (he's listening out
for what his horn wants to skip and shout
miles from the playground
where other kids spin round
in diminishing
circles …) and finishing
a solo many schoolmasters might mark
wrong, because they haven't seen the spark
of genius he tells them he's got.
Which is not
too boastful when you consider
he's the outsider
looking in through the bars
of those imprisoned in themselves
and unable to sever
their ego from their alter ego.
He never
has to wonder who he is – nothing jars
when he starts to blow.
Shelves
of ready-made music clatter
to the floor
unheard by pupils who are wrapped
and still in store
in their desk-bound selves. Having tapped
a hidden barrel, he is breaking
the rules, taking
leave of their senses, imbibing
a home-made brew
they are not privy to.
He's truanting with his horn. I'm describing
his escapes from the norm.
True to form

and a distant memory of lessons, he quotes
in hints, veer
-ing back to the sheer
shape of the tune, it's the combination of notes
that floats him — and us — to another sphere.

Christopher Pilling

DARK BLUES

The bebop of Charlie Parker
has seeds of something darker,
no, not seeds, but the plant entire:
deep black blooms, formed by fire
or the sensation of it in the style —
a singularity. It sucks you in.
And is scalding to the touch, vile
hot licks (vile to the daunted) that win
you with their seductive slippery
snaking. They become a need.
Knowing no-one's hurt by frippery,
whizzing balls-of-the-finger-speed
skip you into a maelstrom of wish-
fulfilment that's close to anguish.
There's nothing trivial about his styl-
ish, sophisticated, prehensile
moods: the fingers' lights, the darks of the runs, the heroin
under your skin
as well as his – he blows and you
turn black and blue
before you can stop

– it's unstoppable – his bebop.

Christopher Pilling

BLUES IN THE NIGHT

for Keith Jafrate

the discovery
of secret sounds
that hide in ice
in the boles
of trees
born
in fierce fires
I am talking
music here
I am talking
the crucible

Milner Place

RHAPSODY IN ICE BLUE

blue blue the misted breath
of saxophones fierce
golden horns ivory
and thick sweet brandy
smiling in the light

soft soft the curling
scent of hair and musk
wild notes burning
crimson night

sweet sweet the lips
a string of pearls
smoking alabaster
wind-blown white

Milner Place

FEVER

Love, love, love
Seven hundred
and seventy seven,
she said

Handed her daughter
the peppermint pack
stamped her foot
shook out a scream
stormed the curtain
and surveyed the crowd

As the spot
picked up
tracked
her right hand

Lazy
finger
click.

Patricia Pogson

A MODERN JAZZ QUARTET

Duke Ellington

Modern? Of course: *Ulysses*
and *The Waste Land* were written
long before *Mood Indigo.*

Though at ease with a keyboard,
pen rather than piano
is your chosen instrument,

the writer's craft replacing
performer's pyrotechnics
in the study's sanctuary:

a poet, substituting
orchestra for typewriter.
I wish I knew the language.

Charlie Parker

Time has distilled these moments,
has sanctified place and date:
Los Angeles, '48,

the point at which suffering
and expertise intersect
in a blues called *Parker's Mood*.

A secret, mysterious
music of purity and
uncanny classicism:

it is clearer now because
unrivalled and unsurpassed,
distilled through a sense of time.

Thelonious Monk

During a tenor solo
at the Royal Festival Hall
you stood up and blew your nose.

The gesture was typical,
the solo was very dull,
and most of us got the point.

So, typically, you find
a perfect absurdity
in the cracks between the keys;

for reverence is no use
to a music which rejects
the gloss of solemnity.

John Coltrane

You managed paradox:
out of certainty you brought
the music of confusion.

Through commitment you had seen
that tone does not carry truth:
one must travel in-between.

There is no perfection here
for each new cluster of notes
diminishes certainty.

One would not have guessed your creed
could be so painfully wrought
into such complexity.

Neil Powell

MOVEMENT IN JAZZ

Tiny pubic hairs litter the bed; hieroglyphs,
little question marks,
poignant scraps of dead life.

I am a scavenger, I lean into the sheets
to catch the scent of what is already past and faint.

You are singing a scat in the shower.
I strain for the glimpses of your voice
in the hiss and and muffle of water.

I strive for sense in your notes
through the same crackling distance of a foreign radio station.

You have been teaching me jazz life,
its relaxed wordlessness,
the threads of ingenuity in the tides of its long wails.

Under the sheets, I listen to a string quartet,
the adagio sticky and sweet on my tongue.

You come back from the shower,
still damp. I lean over to lick your shoulder,
taste the citric tang.
The jazz plays in the background,
circling and questioning, a little sour.

Later, as I make the bed,
I brush the question marks from the sheets,
stretching the cover firm over the mattress,
covering up any gaps.

Kate Scott

FATS WALLER

Ah, Mercy!

You beautiful dead man, still travelling through,
Racing along your wild and cool glissandos,

The Rhythm rocking, holding off, rocking:
Plucked thunders and floating winds. Sweet Thing!

The riffs go climbing through the blue-smoke airs
Of thirty years, of thirty missing years.

Pick us a tune, some old ridiculous song.
Shake it, break it, spin it edge-along,

Tack it up lightly to the trembling wires,
Swoop and clown astride its swinging bars,

Squeeze us your syruped stones through that
Most growly-gay deep voice, you big scat cat:

Hushed honey for sleepy people, a pulled-leg
For those whose aching feet are much too big,

All friendly milkmen and ain't misbehavers.
Croon your dark crotchets and your mocking quavers,

Give us your haunted popcorn yet again,
A crazy sugar that will keep us sane,

A hop-hop-hoppity of wandering chimes
To coax and tease us back to the good times.

Oh patty-cake, patty-cake baker man,
Spin us a perfect circle with each hand.

You died at thirty-nine. Old ivory bones,
You're weaving still those nets of tingling sound.

Ah, Mercy!

Peter Scupham

TO A TWELVE-YEAR-OLD JAZZ FAN

(for George and Margo, and i.m. Chet Baker)

Blurred with coke and fags and booze,
the voice has nothing left to lose.

He rests to let the drums control
the piano-player's fol-de-rol,

bends to Bourbon at his feet
and lights a Lucky, lolls the beat.

You read the inlay cards bare facts:
Chet on trumpet, Stan on sax,

Bond on bass – as tactful as
Charlie Mingus never was –

and for a solo, here he comes,
Connie Kay behind the drums.

Repeat them as you nod your head,
only seconds out of bed.

You mother notes, behind the door,
an off-beat knocking on the floor

and goes to grind a fresh high roast,
light a fag and burn some toast.

George – frankly, wickedness can stem
from playing jazz at six a.m.

It's music, really, for much later.
Much as only tea can cater

for teatime, jazz is only heaven
when played with Mocha after seven.

Fred Sedgwick

DICKIE WELLS SAID: VARIATIONS

1.
'It's only when the crowd deserts
the ballroom we play concerts,
missing the nights swinging and sweating,
serving the dancers in our true setting.
The change isn't our choosing
certainly. We know what we're losing,
we blow different somehow.
It's an imaginary music now.'

2.
In Derry we learnt to love before
we could talk, foxtrotting the floor,
nibbling earlobes
under the spinning crystal globes.
In the ballroom in Bishop Street
the educators of our feet
were James McCafferty's swinging
band and Mick McWilliams singing.

3.
I wish my lovely lucid songs
had the conviction Elton John's
get from just knowing they're wanted.
You have to be good not to be daunted
by indifference, to have the temerity
to play in empty halls for posterity,
for many a valiant old bore
insists on coming back for more.

4.
And of course the old jam sessions!
When work was over we eased tensions
entertaining ourselves and extending the art,
playing wild things, trying parts

we hadn't heard till then.
For the employed ones that was Heaven.
The unemployed were sort of sad,
all jam and no bread.

5.
We're only up here
to give your weddings atmosphere,
to help shy guests rejoice,
to find hidden feelings a voice.
As Jesus said, 'Stuff the applause,
we're here because we're here because
the rat race has gotta swing.
So let's see everybody dancing.'

James Simmons

DIDN'T HE RAMBLE

for Michael Longley

'The family wanted to make a bricklayer of him, but Ferd. Was too smooth and clever a fellow. He preferred to sit in the parlour out of the sun and play piano.'

Henry Morton

There was a hardware shop in Main Street sold
records as well as spades and plastic bowls.
Joe, the assistant, had a taste for jazz.
The shop being empty as it mostly was
I tried out records, then, like seeing the light,
but genuine, I heard Josh White:
I'm going to mo-o-ve you, way on the outskirts of town.
Where was my turntable to set it down!
A voice styled by experience, learning to make

music listening to Blind Willie Blake,
walking the streets of a city, avoiding cops,
toting a cheap guitar and begging box.

The campus poets used to write of saxophones
disgustedly and sneer at gramophones;
but the word of life, if such a thing existed,
was there on record among the rubbish listed
in the catalogues of Brunswick and H.M.V.,
healing the split in sensibility.
Tough reasonableness and lyric grace
together, in poor man's dialect.
Something that no one taught us to expect.
Profundity without the po-face
of court and bourgeois modes. This I could use
to live and die with. Jazz. Blues.
I love the music and the men who made
the music, and instruments they played:
saxophone, piano, trumpet, clarinet,
Bill Broonzy, Armstrong, Basie, Hodges, Chet
Baker, Garner, Tommy Ladnier,
Jelly Roll Morton, Bessie Smith, Bechet,
and Fats Waller, the scholar-clown of song
who sang *Until the Real Thing Comes Along*.
Here was the risen people, their feet
dancing, not out to murder the elite:
'Pardon me, sir, may we be free?
The kitchen staff is having a jamboree.'

History records how people cleared the shelves
of record shops, discovering themselves,
making distinctions in the ordinary,
seeing what they'd been too tired to see;
but most ignored the music. Some were scared,
some greedy, some condemned what they hadn't heard,
some sold cheap imitations, watered it down,
bribed Fats to drink too much and play the clown

instead of the piano, and failed – the man was wise,
he did both painlessly. Jazz is a compromise:
you take the first tune in your head and play
until it's saying what you want to say.
'I ain't got no diplomas,' said Satchmo,
'I look into my heart and blow.'

What if some great ones took to drugs and drink
and killed themselves? Only a boy could think
the world cures easy, and want to blame
someone. I know I'll never be the same.
A mad world my masters! We might have known
that Wardell Gray was only well spoken,
controlled and elegant on saxophone.
He appeared last in a field with his neck broken.
The jazz life did it, not the Ku Klux Klan.
Whatever made the music killed the man.

James Simmons

ONLY A THIMBLEFUL
for Julie London

A thimbleful of a voice, you called it,
lips brushing the microphone
as you began, shimmeringly, to sing.

We slipped into a dream of whispers
meant only for us. A molten mezzo
with a sixty-cigarettes-a-day come-hither voice,

who cried us rivers, through moonless nights,
beneath blue moons. And too good to be true,
you were a face in the misty light,

our Laura of the misty voice who whispered
what we could expect of love: husky words
kept handy, like just-in-case condoms
in inside pockets, sexual IOUs.

Matt Simpson

OLD HANDS
(portrait of a jazz pianist at 80)

They say jazz is a country of the old,
of left-over men, guys with grizzled beards,
plaits or ponytails, out-of-date dudes
with drawled allusions to the hoary
good old days of hip and swing and cool,
cats in awe of cats they learnt from,
the real McCoys that went before.

This piano-man for one looks out of sync,
grey head nodding, answers slow, but still
somehow pert with irony, indulging
his pushy TV questioner. Then wanting
to rattle keys again, saying 'Let me illustrate ...'

So now take two hands in close-up. Not backward
in coming forward. Ten fingers, charged with cunning,
scampering like king crabs racing the tide.

Matt Simpson

EVERYTHING'S DANDY

Billy lays a backbeat down
like a backbone. Rico's burnin' light
with the groove of his trumpet.
'Soul food' Jones earns the rep of his name:
pulls seduction from his bass strings,
then turns up the flame.

Billy's hittin' hide now, with no trace
of apple sauce. Dexter's lickin' ivory
and ebony to tease the crowd.
I'm in the front seat, sittin' on the mood
feelin' for the green light
I'm gonna change to blue.

Solo:

Cleopatra in high heels
with a dress of midnight,
bathing in spotlight milk,
struttin', brazen, butterfly

I could serve the front row
shares between my sheets;
or leave 'em, high and dry
mic lead between their teeth.

Break it down:

As Dexter turns his hurt out to sail on
those white keys and Rico fans the
heartache by blowing regret out to sea,
'til Soul Food plays a phrase
that's the nearest thing to shore
and I carve up a lullaby to share
with the loveless.

Listen:

I'm the silk bird singing out the song
on the horizon, as Billy casts the kitten claw
of snare rooted rhythm, but I'll fly higher,
even in a tiger's eye, for freedom;
my song line high wire for followers to tread.

Are you with me?

'Cos I'm turning out a snake's note
to bareback this backbeat. That sunlight
called trumpet, I mirror with starlight,
in one solid note holding out its own
prayer:

We're alive, baby. We're alive. So, there.

Rommi Smith

GREAT MUSIC

needs fingers, breath and staves
and then that something more, to brim
with clues gripping the listener,
forensically sound so as to identify
the murderer of impossibility.
Bach's fingerprints are all over his
and Mozart bummed his way
onto the photocopier of futurity.
Composers, criminally themselves,
steal the shared secret, worth
more than the world's GNP.

But what of the inspired transient blow
or twitchy fingered strum by those

who perhaps reading no music
keep it together without frame?
They are not similar but the same.
The Great Composer is a shibboleth
if not always a self-cast high romantic statue;
jazz pays its tribute not to that idea
but has equal sound reasons to go on.
With tie loosened, tie quite gone
it drills down into the acquifer:
but here it bubbles out too quick
to build or accrete marble surrounds,
monumentally everlasting or perhaps just *chic.*
Jazz is in real time, the all we've got
but is not opposed to the other lot.
We blow or strum (or those who can do, do),
welling sweet water to get us through.

Michael Standen

THREE SOLOS

BEIDERBECKE

I've packed my bags. Hotel room has gone quiet,
Muddy water rising round the bed,
I count the roses on the wallpaper,
And count the seconds ticking in my head.

The wind is in the east, it whispers brass,
A faint piano tinkles in my cup,
The window light is made of grains of dust
That swirl so thick they choke the music up.

Good luck then boss, and here's another haze
You've got me into, lying flat and cold
As any sheet. Come Gabriel, blow your horn
And turn my dust to silver, if not gold.

WALLER

I was lounging at the Waldorf
with Dr. Hackenbush
and his platinum troupe
of curly chorus girls,
when the night wind muscles in
and gives me a hard push
saying, *Man, don't cast your swine*
before these dainty pearls.
These dainty pearls? I laugh,
My swine will do for all,
my fingers wash them cleaner
than any waterfall.
And I aim the phonograph
at the greasy kitchen wall.

HOLIDAY

A holy day it was, the child was blessed,
I think now of the man that I caressed,
I think now of the men outside the door
The men that sang the blues and knew the score,
The men that could sing holy and sing sweet
Or crude as alley-cats when they're on heat.
I sing the moon, the river and their thirst
But I have had my fill and I could burst.

George Szirtes

JAZZ ON PIANO

In the pub at Sunday lunch
the pianist playing
it's still the same old story
a fight for love and glory
my arm round your shoulder
I told you about Barmouth

1944 when I first saw
                    Casablanca
the pianist plays more jazz
old tunes remembered
and there we go again
                    Redditch
your childhood and adolescence
there   my visits to an aunt
before you were even born
but it doesn't matter
                              age
time passing   only the present
the long moment extended
an endless jazz number
            on the piano.

David Tipton

FOR A JAZZ PIANIST

Seen (through
fogged goggles?)
submerged against
a cellar wall
(of museum dust?
of lumpy porridge?)
where we congest
and thicken (compost
air? scrapyard
breath?) to hear
few bubbled
gritty noises
(patterned?)
from a black

and polished upright
slotted box
(a camel's coffin?)
you (a swaddled
clockwork torso?)
sit before
and prod.

Gael Turnbull

A JAZZ TRUMPETER

Heard once, price of a drink, near empty bar, half a
lifetime away, the tunes gone, like him, but not that grip
of stained fingers, sweat on coiled veins, ballooned cheeks,
clamped mouth, tensed neck, sagged eyes

which maybe saw us, maybe not, their intent not
elsewhere but all there, on what he knew, was about,
whether anyone heard or not, playing, as they say, for all
he was worth.

Gael Turnbull

I FIND AN OLD LETTER

Postmarked Chichester   1pm   17 March 1956
addressed 501493 A.C.2 *myself,*
Hut 160, 17 Flt, 'C' Squdn,
R.A.F. Hednesford, and when she says
she can imagine how I look with my new haircut
all the unnecessary place comes back to me,
the rainswept square that was bashed

by intersecting blue geometries,
corporals bawling their balls off (the overkill
farcical within two weeks); that frantic
camaraderie in homesick huts
and miles of glowering pinewood.

It's a shock being written to from the past
in these phrases jostling with particular life,
zigzag graph of a voice I must strain to catch:
she misses my records and thanks me
for the Kid Ory Oh Didn't He Ramble
and Maryland My Maryland on the other side.
I dive in my tattered pile
Of fifties forty-fives, but I don't have that one.
Did I give her mine, or buy her one?
Whichever way, knowing how Kid, and Bunk,
and Jelly Roll, and Satchmo, and Bix, and Bechet
loomed in that played-out life, I must have thought
something of her. I'd like to hear it again.

But here's the Kid's Dippermouth Blues. I'll
give it a spin. His daintily coarse trombone
still now, for all it blows the blues,
is glad sweet music to my ears.

Hugh Underhill

From MUSIC ON THE WATER. TO BILL COLEMAN IN PARIS

And in neon Paris, Django strummed
his plangent greeting-chords to life
and your horn was at your lips
and sound moved out, Bill, across the water:
flow, Seine, flow, Mississippi,
flow, strangling Rhine!

Et nous, les os, devenons cendre et pouldre

And I, in by-passed England, rain on the window,
spin your records and groove down the centuries
hearing the creak of axles and the crack of whips
the murmur of women to their shawled babies.

The deep lanes of Europe: the sharks rising
to the unchained corpses: the uncatchable carp
in the *rusée* Seine, knowing all men's tricks:
knowing men to their depths, in the agony
of unillusion, as the whores
know them in the tall, scented houses,
as slaves in their patience know them
unbuttoned, unmasked, yet hung about with dreams
like mad vines swaying in the tropic night
huge flowers that when we touch them turn to scabs.

Bill, my friend, courteous and smiling,
my tall unruffled uncle, at ease in restaurants,
king of the world of easy handshakes,
anchored to Swiss Lily like a bronze statue
on a marble plinth, you know all this:

you and the gipsy Django sang it all.

And now that he is dead, you sing it still.
The night stirs the dark vines, the enslaved eyes
stare on the naked face of pitiable huge Man,

and sound, always your sound, moves out across the water.

John Wain

JOYSPRING

Fat Buddha nods, his girls
migrate their sweet virginities;
the graveyards freshen up & dance
& skinny Yogis mutter ... but,
their smiles! ... their smiles!

Clifford Brown & Harold Land
with music, silver, lean with joy,
you stroll through ivory
admonishing a blossom!
pursue a melody across
an algebra of sun & shade: a rhythm!

Brownie dead at 26, his Spring.
Harold gigs around, they say. I hear
the Spring go by as shortly as a dance
& all your graces call...
the flowers!... the flowers!

John Hartley Williams

IT'S THE UNWEPT TEARS...

i.m. Albert Nicholas, clarinettist

It's the unwept tears I like
in the song *Farewell to the Moth*,
written by Sam Feral and Bunny Marmoset,
those two lyrical wolfhounds,
their ferocious clarity of phrasing
a lighthouse sweeping circles
over the nothing typhooning out there,
sinking ships,
and anything else you can think of,
though I'm not particularly thinking,
nuzzling a second glass of *Veterano*,

enjoying its harmony
with anchovy-stuffed olives, and
absent-mindedly attentive to you Albert,
the piping desolation of your high notes,
the gruff scrape of your bass.
Your circling strobe is nothing less
than the dark's animadversion.
You and the brandy sips.
But in between the rays I glimpse
things slipping past me
from the cryptic world of undoing.
Who are those enraged Pharisees,
crawling under the wires of lights,
to occupy the shadysides
of sunny streets?
Try another olive, John.
Another slurp, with something like
the breathy drizzling sound, Albert,
you make at the end of a chorus.
Ignore the phantoms.

And so, ignoring them,
I gaze at a lamp-attracted moth
bouncing blindly off the wall
just beyond the flicker of a gecko's tongue.
The gecko darts.
The moth takes a turn
no free molecule would dream of.
The gecko stops dead.
Missed.
If the universe has a brain somewhere,
that moth
is outside the universe completely.
And you, Albert – laying down
the freest of airy lines –
your *obbligato* to the bumptious world
makes floating counterpoise

to the dust-fevered
who mire the light.
You send old Crazywing
colliding off towards another candle.
Your sonorous contralto
quivers to its coda.
The olives are finished. So is the brandy.
The player clicks on to repeat.
The light rays start their sweep again through nothing.
And the gecko doesn't move for hours.

John Hartley Williams

THE PIANO PLAYER

derby hat
& bootlace tie
I'll play this jazz
until you die

don't you worry
don't you fret
if jazz ain't been
invented yet

in a minute
(small excuse)
all around me
hell breaks loose

walls collapsing
bullets flying
i can't stop
folk from dying

music is their
crowd improver
what they need's
a party mover

background music
fast & vile
lends each moment
sort of style

at my back
the place is zero
smashed to blazes
save the hero

on his face
it slowly dawns
thru my hat
protrude two horns!

o come along
& listen to
Infernal Rag!
Satanic Blues!

John Hartley Williams

ACKNOWLEDGEMENTS

to POETRY NOTTINGHAM for C.J. Allen's "Sonny Rollins on the Williamsburg Bridge"; to PENGUIN BOOKS for "Farewell Blues" Copyright © 1979 Kingsley Amis. Reprinted by kind permission of Jonathan Clowes Ltd., London, on behalf of the Literary Estate of Kingsley Amis; Roger Burford Mason's "Three for the Duke" first appeared in SOLOS, Dodman Press, 1985; to CONFESSIONS OF AN OLD BELIEVER (1996) and TAKE IT EASY (2003), both Redbeck Press, for poems by Jim Burns; the poems by Derrick Buttress appeared, in order, in the journals MAGMA, THE PENNILESS PRESS and WOW; "Glassblower" by Peter Carpenter was first published in NO AGE, Shoestring Press, (2001); "For a Cornet Player, Retired" by Barry Cole first appeared in CRITICAL SURVEY; John Cotton's two poems first appeared in SOLOS; Simon Darragh's "The Musicians" was first published in FOREIGN CORRESPONDENCE, Peterloo Poets (2000); to STAND for Douglas Dunn's "The Jazz Orchestra", and Faber & Faber Ltd. For permission to use "Billie 'n' Me, from THE HAPPIER LIFE (1972); to Bloodaxe Books for Roy Fisher's "The Thing About Joe Sullivan" and "The Home Pianist's Companion"; Michael Foley's Elegy for Thelonious" was first published in INSOMNIA IN THE AFTERNOON, Blackstaff Press, 1994; John Gohorry's "Mr. Acker Bilk" was first published in SOLOS; "Chet Baker" and "Ghost of a Chance" by John Harvey were first published in GHOSTS OF A CHANCE, Smith/Doorstop Books, 1992; Geoffrey Holloway's "Band Call" first appeared in OSTINATO as did "Three Singers" by James Kirkup; Jazzbo Le Griot, by M.K.E. Lange was first published in IN CONTEXT, NSROMA Publications, (n.d.); Philip Larkin's "For Sidney Bechet" was first published in THE WHITSUN WEDDINGS, Faber & Faber, 1963; Michael Longley's "Words for Jazz Perhaps" and "Doctor Jazz" are from POEMS 1963–1983, Salamander Press, 1985, and "Jug Band" from GORSE FIRES, Secker & Warburg, 1991; John Lucas's "Strolling" was first published in ONE FOR THE PIANO, Redbeck Press (1997), "Fats at the BBC" and "Tales from the (English) Jazz Age" both come from A WORLD PERHAPS: NEW AND SELECTED POEMS, Sow's Ear Press/Trent Books, 2000; the poems by Alexis Lykiard are taken from LIVING JAZZ, The Tenormen Press, 1991; Sue May's "Avogadro's Number" first appeared in OSTINATO; the three poems by Peter McSloy were first published in FOR JAZZ; TWENTY ONE SONNETS, hit & run press, (USA 1995); Adrian Mitchell's poems are all from POEMS, 1953–1984. Bloodaxe (1997) apart from "Deep Purple Wine", which comes from BLUE COFFEE: POEMS 1985–1996, Bloodaxe (1996); John Mole's "Listening" comes from SELECTED POEMS, Sinclair Stevenson (1995), "Benny Goodman"from DEPENDING ON THE LIGHT, Peterloo Poets (1993), "Wild Bill" from FOR THE MOMENT, Peterloo Poets (2000); Graham Mort's "A Signalman Hears Jazz" was first published in A COUNTRY ON FIRE, Littlewood Press (1986); Sean O'Brien's "Jazz" was first published in THE INDOOR PARK, Bloodaxe, 1983; Neil Powell's "A Modern Jazz Quartet" was first published in TRUE COLOURS, Carcanet Press, 1991; "Movement in Jazz" by Kate Scott was first published in STITCHES, Peterloo Poets (2003); Peter Scupham's "Fats Waller" comes from his COLLECTED POEMS, Carcanet Press (2002); the poems by James Simmons are from POEMS 1956-1986, Bloodaxe (1986); Rommi Smith's "Fine and Dandy" first appeared in SMOKE; "Three Solos" by George Szirtes was first published in SOLOS; "Jazz on Piano" by David Tipton was first published in AMULET AGAINST THE EVIL EYE AND OTHER POEMS, Salzburg (1997); Gael Turnbull's "For a Jazz Pianist" comes from A GATHERING OF POEMS, 1950–1980, Anvil Press, 1983; the excerpt from "Music on the Water: to Bill Coleman in Paris" is from John Wain's LETTERS TO FIVE ARTISTS, Macmillan (1969). "The Piano Player"by John Hartley Williams was first published in BRIGHT RIVER YONDER, Bloodaxe Books (1987). "It's the Unwept Tears", from BLUES, published by Jonathan Cape, 2004. Reprinted by permission of the Random House Group Ltd. All other Copyrights lie with the authors.

OTHER BOOKS FROM SHOESTRING PRESS

POEMS Manolis Anagnostakis. Translated into English by Philip Ramp. A wide ranging selection from a poet who is generally regarded as one of Greece's most important living poets and who in 1985 won the Greek State Prize for Poetry.
ISBN 1 899549 19 6 £8.95

HALF WAY TO MADRID: POEMS Nadine Brummer *Poetry Book Society Recommendation.*
ISBN 1 899549 70 6 £7.50

BROXTOWE BOY: A MEMOIR Derrick Buttress. ISBN 1 899549 98 6 £8.95

PASTORAL: POEMS Philip Callow. ISBN 1 904886 06 X £8.95

TESTIMONIES: NEW AND SELECTED POEMS Philip Callow. With Introduction by Stanley Middleton. A generous selection which brings together work from all periods of the career of this acclaimed novelist, poet and biographer. ISBN 1 899549 44 7 £8.95

Shoestring Press also publish Philip Callow's novel, BLACK RAINBOW.
ISBN 1 899549 33 1 £6.99

TARO FAIR Ian Caws. ISBN 1 899549 80 3 £7.50

THE WEIGHT OF COWS Mandy Coe. ISBN 1 899549 97 8 £7.95

INSIDE OUTSIDE: NEW AND SELECTED POEMS Barry Cole. "A fine poet ... the real thing." *Stand.* ISBN 1 899549 11 0 £6.95

GHOSTS ARE PEOPLE TOO Barry Cole. ISBN 1 899549 93 5 £6.00

SELECTED POEMS Tassos Denegris. Translated into English by Philip Ramp. A generous selection of the work of a Greek poet with an international reputation.
ISBN 1 899549 45 9 £6.95

WHO: Alan Dent. ISBN 1 904886 07 8 £8.95

THE NEW GIRLS Sue Dymoke. ISBN 1 904886 00 0 £7.95

COLLECTED POEMS Ian Fletcher. With Introduction by Peter Porter. Fletcher's work is that of "a virtuoso", as Porter remarks, a poet in love with "the voluptuousness of language" who is also a master technician. ISBN 1 899549 22 6 £8.95

LAUGHTER FROM THE HIVE Kate Foley. ISBN 1 904886 01 9 £7.95

THE HOME KEY John Greening. ISBN 1 899549 92 7 £8.95

KAVITA TF Griffin. ISBN 1 899549 85 4 £6.50

LONG SHADOWS: POEMS 1957–2000 JC Hall. ISBN 1 899549 26 9 £8.95

A PLACE APART Stuart Henson. ISBN 1 899549 95 1 £7.95

CRAEFT: POEMS FROM THE ANGLO-SAXON Translated and with Introduction and notes by Graham Holderness. *Poetry Book Society Recommendation.*
ISBN 1 899549 67 6 £7.50

ODES Andreas Kalvos. Translated into English by George Dandoulakis. The first English version of the work of a poet who is in some respects the equal of his contemporary, Greece's national poet, Solomos. ISBN 1 899549 21 8 £9.95

OMM SETY John Greening. ISBN 1 899549 51 X £5.95

FIRST DOG Nikos Kavvadias. Translated into English by Simon Darragh.
ISBN 1 899549 73 0 £7.95

A COLD SPELL Angela Leighton. *Other Poetry*. ISBN 1 899549 40 4 £6.95

WISING UP, DRESSING DOWN: POEMS Edward Mackinnon.
ISBN 1 899549 66 8 £6.95

ELSEWHERE Michael Murphy. ISBN 1 899549 87 0 £7.95

TOUCHING DOWN IN UTOPIA: POEMS Hubert Moore.
ISBN 1 899549 68 4 £6.95 Second Printing

MORRIS PAPERS: POEMS Arnold Rattenbury. Includes 5 colour illustrations of Morris's wallpaper designs. *Poetry Nation Review.* ISBN 1 899549 03 X £4.95

MAKING SENSE Nigel Pickard. ISBN 1 899549 94 3 £6.00

THE ISLANDERS: POEMS Andrew Sant. ISBN 1 899549 72 2 £7.50

BEHIND THE LINES Vernon Scannell. ISBN 1 9004886 02 7 £8.95

MEDAL FOR MALAYA: a novel David Tipton. ISBN 1899549 75 7 £7.95

PARADISE OF EXILES: a novel David Tipton. ISBN 1899549 34 X £6.99

STONELAND HARVEST: NEW AND SELECTED POEMS Dimitris Tsaloumas. This generous selection brings together poems from all periods of Tsaloumas's life and makes available for the first time to a UK readership the work of this major Greek-Australian poet.
ISBN 1 8995549 35 8 £8.00

AT THE EDGE OF LIGHT Lynne Wycherley. ISBN 1 899549 89 7 £7.95

TAKE FIVE: poems by Ann Atkinson, Michael Bartholomew-Biggs, Malcolm Carson, George Parfitt, and Deborah Tyler-Bennett. ISBN 1 899549 90 0 £7.95

For full catalogue write to:
Shoestring Press
19 Devonshire Avenue
Beeston, Nottingham, NG9 1BS UK
or visit us on www.shoestringpress.co.uk